Ages 5 and Up

Alfred's Kid's Piano Course Complete

The Easiest Piano Method Ever!

Christine H. Barden • Gayle Kowalchyk • E. L. Lancaster

Alfred Alfred Music
P.O. Box 10003
Van Nuys, CA 91410-0003
alfred.com

ISBN-10: 1-4706-3307-8 (Book & Online Audio)
ISBN-13: 978-1-4706-3307-3 (Book & Online Audio)

ISBN-10: 1-4706-3306-X (Book, DVD & Online Video/Audio)
ISBN-13: 978-1-4706-3306-6 (Book, DVD & Online Video/Audio)

Cover and interior illustrations by Jeff Shelly.

Alfred Cares. Contents printed on
environmentally responsible paper.

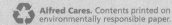

Contents

Online audio is included that contains all the songs in the book, so you may listen and play along with them. An audio icon beside the title of each song shows two track numbers. The first track number is for the kid's part alone, and the second track number is for the kid's part with a colorful accompaniment. Above each audio icon, the original book number is indicated so that when you access the MP3 tracks, they are conveniently organized by book in separate locations.

The online audio can be streamed on your computer, smart phone, or tablet and can also be downloaded for off-line use. Follow the instructions on the inside front cover to access the audio.

How to Sit at the Piano

To play well, it is important to sit correctly at the piano. Follow the instructions on this page so you are playing with good posture and hand position. You will also learn to sit at the correct height on the bench and at the right distance from the keyboard.

- Sit tall!
- Let your arms hang loosely from your shoulders.
- Place the bench facing the piano squarely.
- Keep your knees slightly under the keyboard.

If you are small:

- Sit on a book or cushion.

If your feet don't touch the floor:

- Place a book or stool under your feet.

Curve Your Fingers!

Always curve your fingers when you play.

1. Practice pretending to hold a bubble in your hand.
2. Shape your hand and hold the bubble gently, so that it doesn't pop.
3. Use this hand position on the keyboard.

Left Hand Finger Numbers

Fingers are given numbers for playing the piano. The thumb is finger 1, and pinky is finger 5. Memorize the numbers of all your fingers.

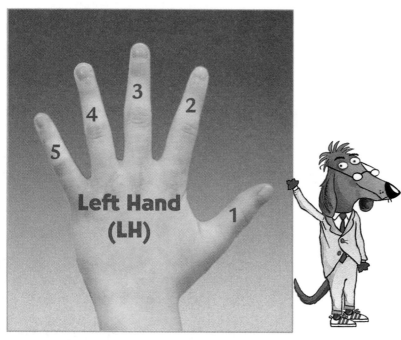

Hold up your **left hand** and wiggle each finger:

- Finger 1 (Thumbkin)
- Finger 2 (Pointer)
- Finger 3 (Tall Man)
- Finger 4 (Ring Man)
- Finger 5 (Pinky)

Activity

Draw an outline of your left hand in the space below and number each finger.

Right Hand Finger Numbers

The fingers of the right hand are numbered the same way as the left hand. Put your hands together, with fingers touching, and steadily tap finger 1 of both hands against each other. Then tap together finger 2 of both hands, then finger 3, finger 4, and finger 5.

Hold up your **right hand** and wiggle each finger:

- Finger 1 (Thumbkin)
- Finger 2 (Pointer)
- Finger 3 (Tall Man)
- Finger 4 (Ring Man)
- Finger 5 (Pinky)

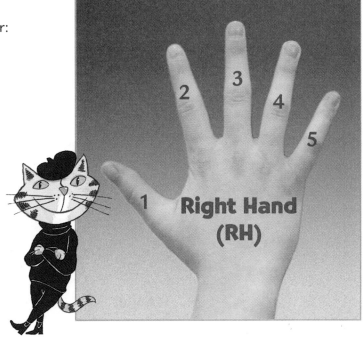

Right Hand (RH)

Activity

Draw an outline of your right hand in the space below and number each finger.

ACTIVITY:
Left Hand Finger Numbers

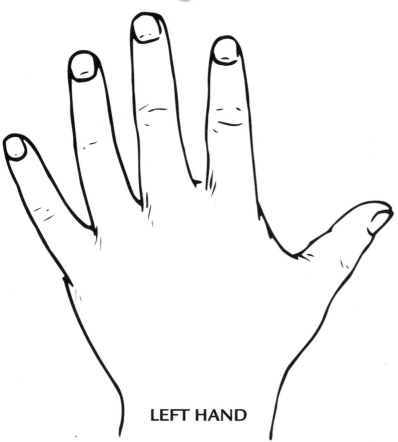

LEFT HAND

1. Color finger 1 red.
2. Color finger 2 blue.
3. Color finger 3 purple.
4. Color finger 4 green.
5. Color finger 5 brown.

ACTIVITY:
Right Hand Finger Numbers

1. Color finger 1 red.
2. Color finger 2 blue.
3. Color finger 3 purple.
4. Color finger 4 green.
5. Color finger 5 brown.

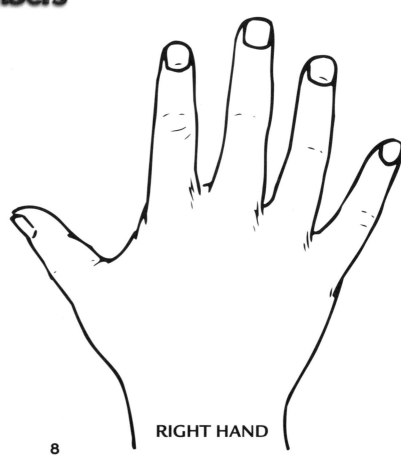

RIGHT HAND

The Keyboard

The keyboard has white keys and black keys. The keys on the left side of the keyboard make low sounds. The keys on the right make high sounds.

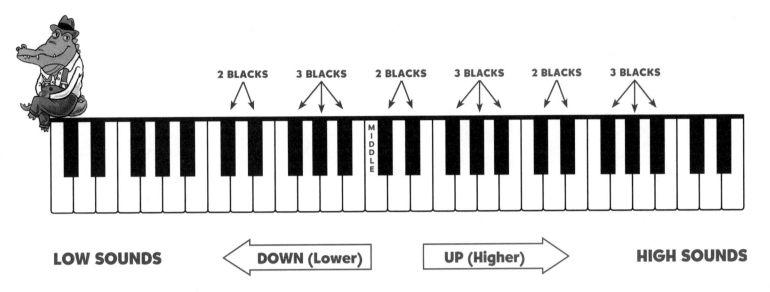

2 BLACKS   3 BLACKS   2 BLACKS   3 BLACKS   2 BLACKS   3 BLACKS

LOW SOUNDS   ← DOWN (Lower)   UP (Higher) →   HIGH SOUNDS

Two-Black-Key Groups

Two-black-key groups are easy to find. Count the number of two-black-key groups on your keyboard.

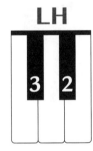

LH

Using LH fingers 2 and 3 together, begin at the middle of the keyboard and play both notes of each two-black-key group going down to the bottom of the keyboard.

Do the sounds get **higher** or **lower**?_____

RH

Using RH fingers 2 and 3 together, begin at the middle of the keyboard and play both notes of each two-black-key group going up to the top of the keyboard.

Do the sounds get **higher** or **lower**?

_____

Three-Black-Key Groups

Three-black-key groups alternate with two-black-key groups. Count the number of three-black-key groups on your keyboard.

LH

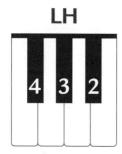

Using LH fingers 2, 3, and 4 together, begin at the middle of the keyboard and play all three notes of each three-black-key group going down to the bottom of the keyboard.

Do the sounds get **higher** or **lower**?_____

RH

Using RH fingers 2, 3, and 4 together, begin at the middle of the keyboard and play all three notes of each three-black-key group going up to the top of the keyboard.

Do the sounds get **higher** or **lower**?_____

Activity

1. Circle each group of two black keys.

2. Draw a box around each group of three black keys.

ACTIVITY:
Two- and Three- Black Key Groups

- Circle each two-black-key group with a **blue** crayon.
- Circle each three-black-key group with a **red** crayon.

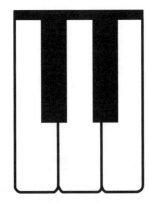
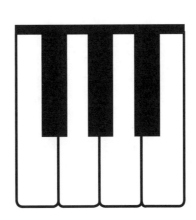

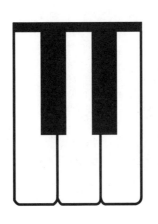
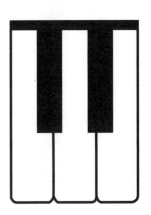

Playing Two Black Keys

Symbols that show how loud or soft to play are called **dynamics**. These symbols come from Italian words.

Loud Sounds

f

The sign f stands for *forte*, which means to play **loud**.

Using LH fingers 2 and 3, play two black keys **low** on the keyboard at once. Play the two keys loudly (f) on each word as you say,

"I can play two low black keys."

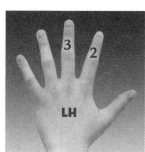

LH

Soft Sounds

p

The sign p stands for *piano*, which means to play **soft**.

Using RH fingers 2 and 3, play two black keys **high** on the keyboard at once. Play the two keys softly (p) on each word as you say,

"I can play two high black keys."

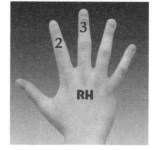

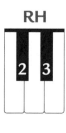

RH

Using fingers 2 and 3 of either hand, play **all** the two-black-key groups on the entire keyboard.

Quarter Note

Introducing the Quarter Note

Each quarter note has a round black circle called a **notehead** with a line called a **stem**.

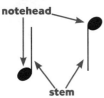

A **quarter note** gets **one** count.

Count: 1   1   1   1

Bar lines divide the music into equal ***measures.***

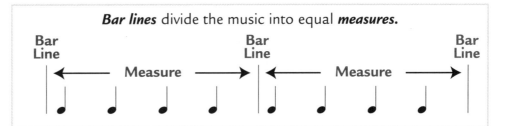

Practice Directions

Now it is time to play your first pieces on the keyboard. Follow these practice directions.

1. Point to the quarter notes in the songs below and count aloud evenly.

2. Play one key at a time and say the finger numbers.

3. Play and sing the words.

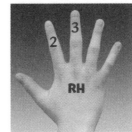

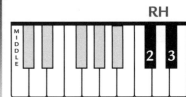

Book 1
Track 1 (45)

Right Hand Marching

DOUBLE BAR used at the end

Count: 1   1   1   1   1   1   1   1
        Right   hand   march -   ing   2   3   2   3

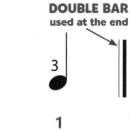

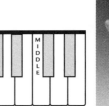
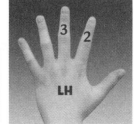

Book 1
Track 2 (46)

Left Hand Walking

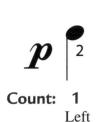  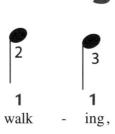

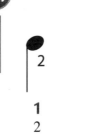  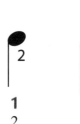 

Count: 1   1   1   1   1   1   1   1
        Left   hand   walk -   ing,   2   3   2   3

13

ACTIVITY: The Quarter Note

A *quarter note* has a black notehead and a stem. Each quarter note gets one count.

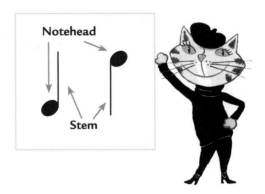

How to Draw Quarter Notes

Step 1: Create noteheads by tracing the ovals and coloring them black.

Step 2: Create the stems. For the first three notes, trace the lines going down from the left of the noteheads. For the second three notes, trace the stems going up from the right of the noteheads.

Draw four more quarter notes with stems going down.

Draw four more quarter notes with stems going up.

Loud and Soft Sounds

1. The sign *p (piano)* means to play
    loud.
    soft.
    circle one

2. The sign *f (forte)* means to play
    loud.
    soft.
    circle one

Playing Three Black Keys

When playing the three black keys, remember to play loud for f and soft for p.

 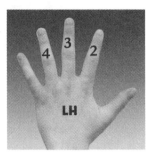

Using LH fingers 2, 3, and 4, play three black keys **low** on the keyboard at once. Play the three keys softly (p) on each word as you say,

"I can play three low black keys."

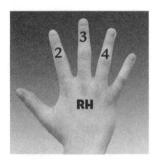 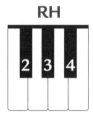

Using RH fingers 2, 3, and 4, play three black keys **high** on the keyboard at once. Play the three keys loudly (f) on each word as you say,

"I can play three high black keys."

Using fingers 2, 3, and 4 of either hand, play **all** the three-black-key groups on the entire keyboard.

Quarter Rest

Introducing the Quarter Rest

Rests are signs of **silence**. They tell you to lift your hand to stop the sound.

A *quarter rest*

𝄽

gets **one** count.

Practice Directions
Follow the practice directions on page 13 as you play these pieces.

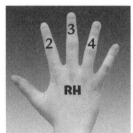

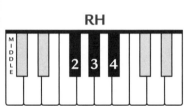

A Mouse's Melody

Book 1
Track 3 (47)

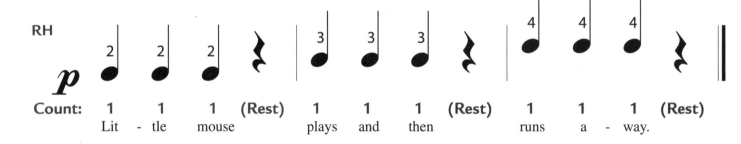

Count:	1	1	1	(Rest)	1	1	1	(Rest)	1	1	1	(Rest)
	Lit	- tle	mouse		plays	and	then		runs	a	- way.	

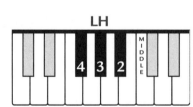

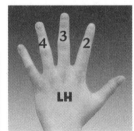

A Bear's Song

Book 1
Track 4 (48)

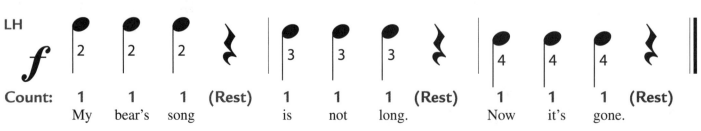

Count:	1	1	1	(Rest)	1	1	1	(Rest)	1	1	1	(Rest)
	My	bear's	song		is	not	long.		Now	it's	gone.	

ACTIVITY:
The Quarter Rest

Quarter Rest

The 𝄽 means to be silent for one count.

How to Draw Quarter Rests

Step 1: Trace the short lines slanting down from left to right.

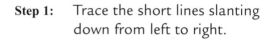

Step 2: Trace the longer lines slanting down from right to left.

Step 3: Trace the other short lines slanting down from left to right.

Step 4: Trace the curled lines, almost like a letter "c."

Draw four more quarter rests.

Black-Key Groups

1. This is a two-three- black-key group.

   circle one

2. This is a two-three- black-key group.

   circle one

Half Note

Introducing the Half Note

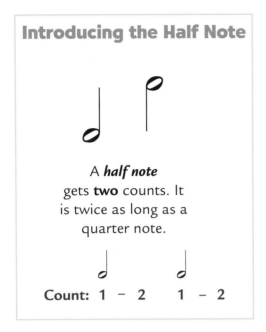

A *half note* gets **two** counts. It is twice as long as a quarter note.

Count: 1 – 2   1 – 2

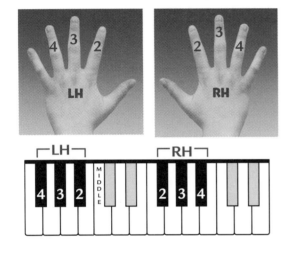

Practice Directions

Follow the practice directions on page 13 as you play "Hot Cross Buns."

The right hand plays the top line, and the left hand plays the bottom line.

Hot Cross Buns

Book 1
Track 5 (49)

RH

f

Count: 1   1   1 - 2   1   1   1 - 2   1   1   1   1   1   1   1 - 2

Hot cross buns! Hot cross buns! Yum - my, yum - my, hot cross buns!

LH

Count: 1   1   1 - 2   1   1   1 - 2   1   1   1   1   1   1   1 - 2

Hot cross buns! Hot cross buns! Yum - my, yum - my, hot cross buns!

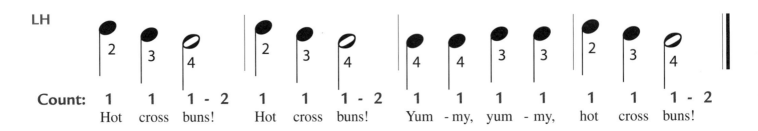

ACTIVITY: The Half Note

A *half note* gets two counts. It is twice as long as a quarter note.

How to Draw Half Notes

Step 1:   Create noteheads by tracing the ovals

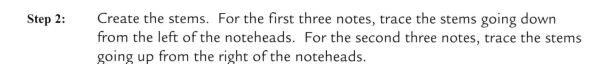

Step 2:   Create the stems. For the first three notes, trace the stems going down from the left of the noteheads. For the second three notes, trace the stems going up from the right of the noteheads.

Draw four more half notes with stems going down.

Draw four more half notes with stems going up.

19

Whole Note

Introducing the Whole Note

𝐨

A **whole note** gets **four** counts. It is as long as two half notes or four quarter notes.

Count: 1 – 2 – 3 – 4

Practice Directions

Follow the practice directions on page 13 as you play "Old MacDonald Had a Farm." The right hand alternates with the left hand on each line.

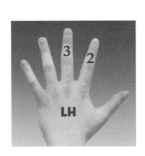
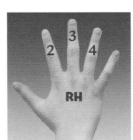

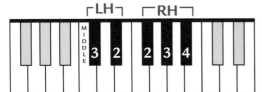

Old MacDonald Had a Farm

Book 1
Track 6 (50)

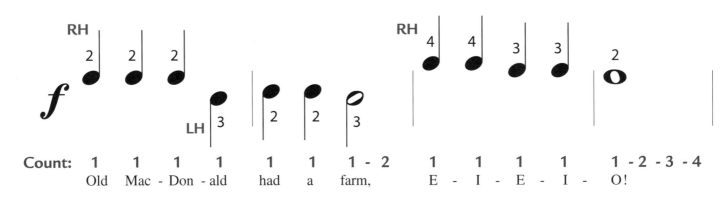

Count: 1   1   1   1   1   1   1 - 2   1   1   1   1   1 - 2 - 3 - 4
Old Mac - Don - ald   had   a   farm,   E - I - E - I - O!

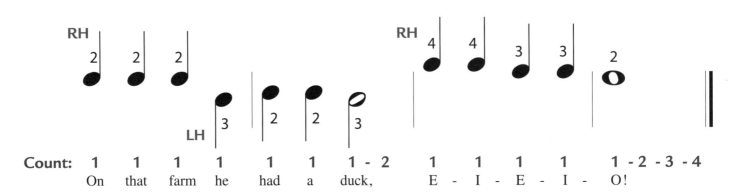

Count: 1   1   1   1   1   1   1 - 2   1   1   1   1   1 - 2 - 3 - 4
On   that farm he   had   a   duck,   E - I - E - I - O!

20

ACTIVITY: The Whole Note

A *whole note* gets four counts.

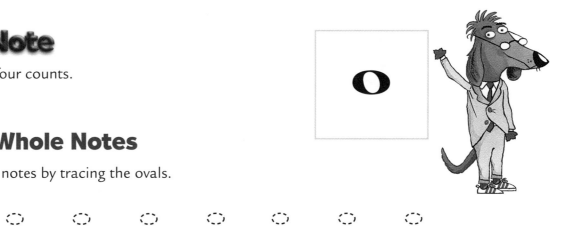

How to Draw Whole Notes

Create whole notes by tracing the ovals.

𝐨   ⬭   ⬭   ⬭   ⬭   ⬭   ⬭   ⬭

Note Review

1. Circle the name of each note. Then write the number of counts it gets on the blank line.

	Circle the note name:	Number of counts:
	quarter note **half note**	_____
	quarter note **whole note**	_____
	half note **whole note**	_____

2. Circle each whole note with a **green** crayon.
    Circle each half note with a **blue** crayon.
    Circle each quarter note with a **red** crayon.

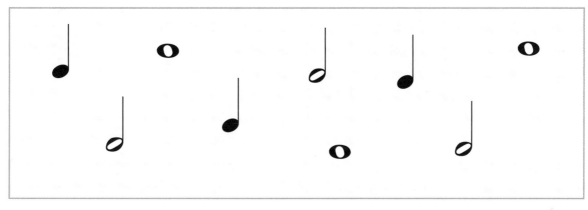

White Keys

The white keys are named for the first seven letters of the alphabet:

A B C D E F G

The lowest key on the keyboard is A.

The highest key on the keyboard is C.

LOW

HIGH

Middle C

Did You Notice?
The key names are used over and over!

Write the name of each white key on the keyboard below.

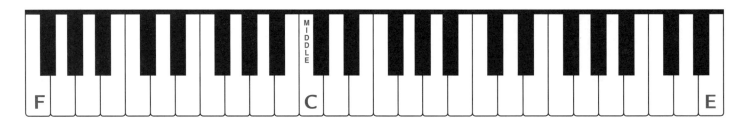

F

MIDDLE C

E

ACTIVITY: White Keys

Piano keys are named for the first seven letters of the alphabet.

A   B   C   D   E   F   G

1. Write the missing letter names from the music alphabet on each line.

   - **A**   ___   **C**   ___   **E**   ___   **G**
   - ___   **B**   ___   ___   **E**   **F**   ___

2. Write the name of every white key on the keyboard, beginning with the given A.

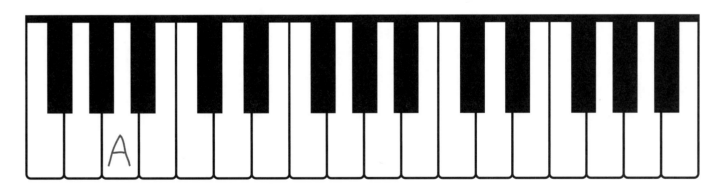

3. Write the letter name on each key marked X.

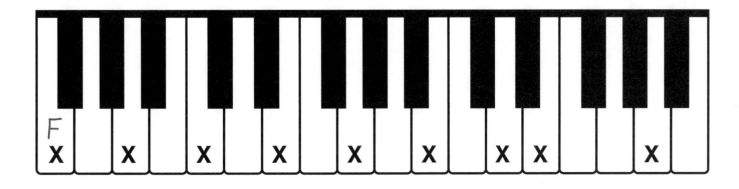

Finding D on the Keyboard

D is the white key in the middle of a two-black-key group.

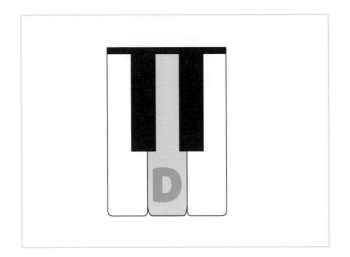

Find each D on the keyboard below and color it yellow.

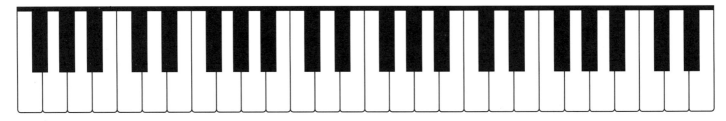

Practice Directions

1. Clap (or tap) and count aloud evenly.
2. Point to the notes and rests and count aloud evenly.
3. Play and sing the words.

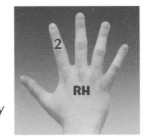

Use finger 2 (Pointer) to play each D in "The D Song."

The D Song

Book 1
Track 7 (51)

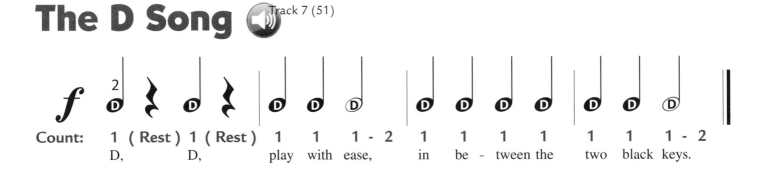

Count:	1	(Rest)	1	(Rest)	1	1	1 - 2	1	1	1	1	1	1	1 - 2
	D,		D,		play	with	ease,	in	be -	tween the		two	black	keys.

Finding C on the Keyboard

C is the white key to the left of a two-black-key group.

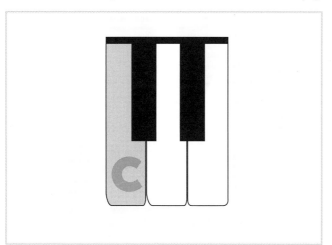 

Find each C on the keyboard below and color it green.

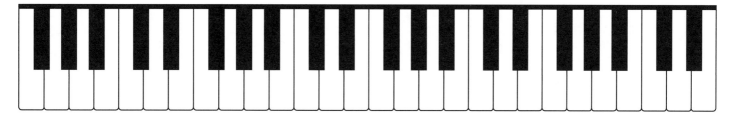

Practice Directions
Follow the practice directions on page 24 as you play "The C Song." Use finger 1 (Thumbkin) to play each C.

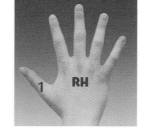 

The C Song
Book 1
 Track 8 (52)

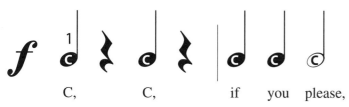 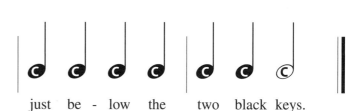

C,   C,   if   you please,   just be - low   the   two black keys.

Finding E on the Keyboard

E is the white key to the right of a two-black-key group.

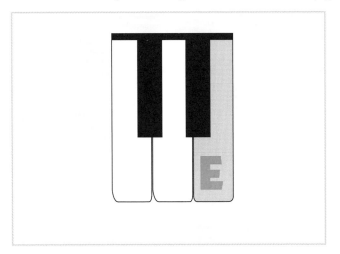

Find each E on the keyboard below and color it red.

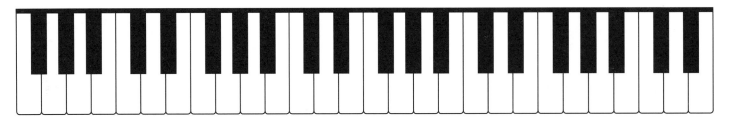

Practice Directions

Follow the practice directions on page 24 as you play "The E Song." Use finger 3 (Tall Man) to play each E.

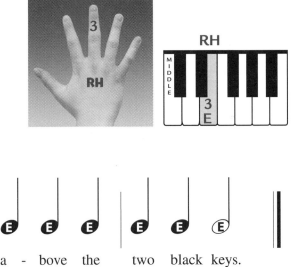

The E Song

Book 1
Track 9 (53)

E,   E,   look for me.   I'm a - bove the   two   black keys.

ACTIVITY:
Finding C, D, and E on the Keyboard

1. Color the HIGHEST C **green.**
2. Color the LOWEST C **purple.**
3. Color the other C's **brown.**

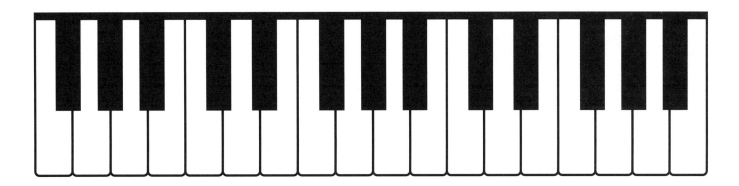

4. Color the HIGHEST D **red.**
5. Color the LOWEST D **yellow.**
6. Color the other D's **blue.**

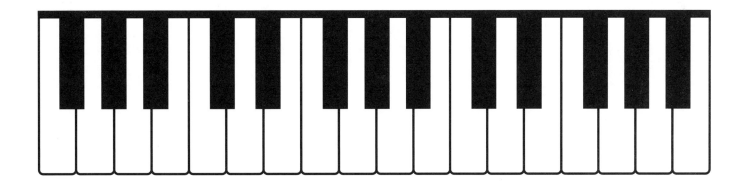

7. Color the HIGHEST E **pink.**
8. Color the LOWEST E **orange.**
9. Color the other E's **green.**

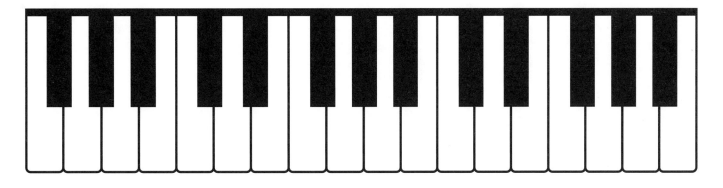

Practice Directions

1. Clap (or tap) and count aloud evenly.
2. Point to the notes and rests and count aloud evenly.
3. Say the finger numbers aloud while playing the notes in the air.
4. Play and say the finger numbers.
5. Play and say the note names.
6. Play and sing the words.

"Go Tell Aunt Rhody" for right hand uses fingers 1, 2, and 3.

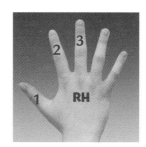

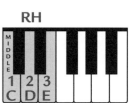

Go Tell Aunt Rhody (for RH)

Book 1
Track 10 (54)

Count: 1 - 2   1   1   1 - 2   1 - 2   1 - 2   1   1   1   1   1 - 2
Go   tell   Aunt   Rho   -   dy,   go   tell   Aunt   Rho   -   dy,

Skip 2 on D

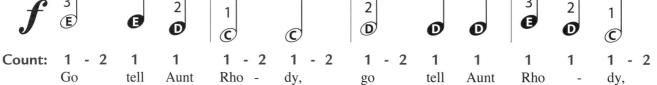

Count: 1 - 2   1   1   1 - 2   1   1   1   1   1   1   1 - 2 - 3 - 4
go   tell   Aunt   Rho   -   dy,   get   up,   get   out   of   bed.

Practice Directions

Follow the practice directions on page 28.

After you have learned to play "Go Tell Aunt Rhody" on both pages 28 and 29, play them without stopping in between to create a longer song.

"Go Tell Aunt Rhody" for left hand uses fingers 3 on C, 2 on D, and 1 on E.

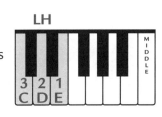

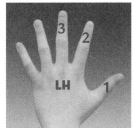

Book 1
Track 11 (55)

Go Tell Aunt Rhody (for LH)

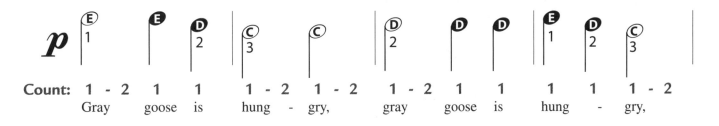

Count: 1 - 2   1   1   1 - 2   1 - 2   1 - 2   1   1   1   1   1 - 2
Gray   goose   is   hung - gry,   gray   goose   is   hung - gry,

Skip 2 on D

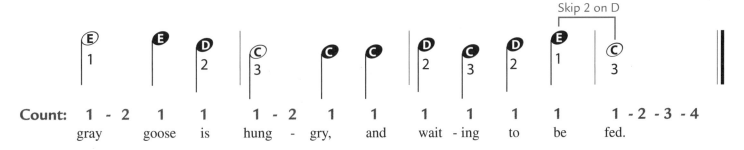

Count: 1 - 2   1   1   1 - 2   1   1   1   1   1   1   1 - 2 - 3 - 4
gray   goose   is   hung - gry,   and   wait - ing   to   be   fed.

29

Review: C, D, E

Draw a line from each key marked with an "X" in the first column to its note name in the second column.

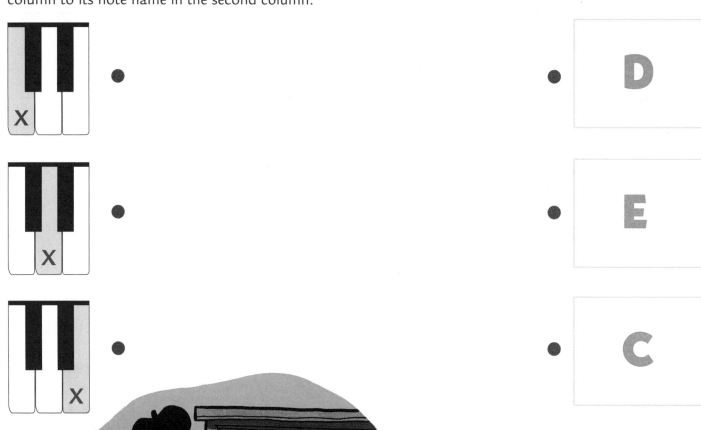

D

E

C

Practice Directions
Follow the practice directions on page 24 as you play "The C Song, Again!" Use left hand finger 1 (Thumbkin) to play each C.

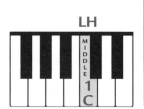

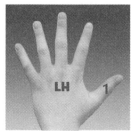

The C Song, Again!

Book 1
Track 12 (56)

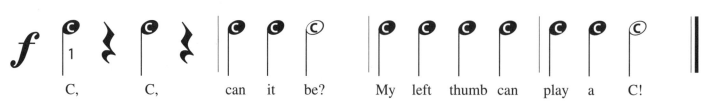

C,   C,   can   it   be?   My   left   thumb   can   play   a   C!

Finding B on the Keyboard

B is to the right of a three-black-key group.

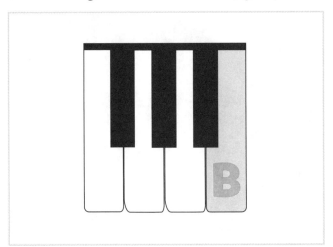

Find each B on the keyboard below and color it purple.

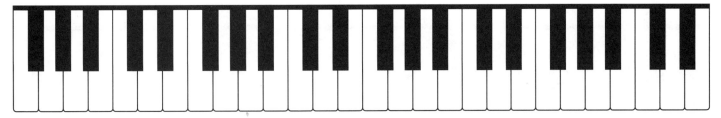

Practice Directions

Follow the practice directions on page 24 as you play "The B Song." Use left hand finger 2 (Pointer) to play each B.

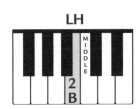

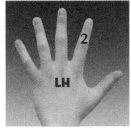

The B Song

Book 1
Track 13 (57)

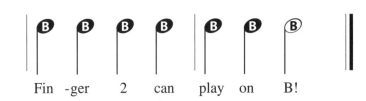

B,   B,   look at me!   Fin - ger 2 can play on B!

Finding A on the Keyboard

A is the white key to the left of B.

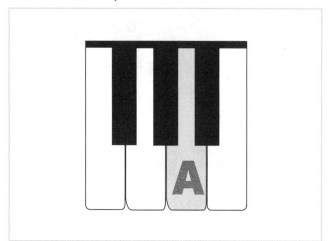

Find each A on the keyboard below and color it blue.

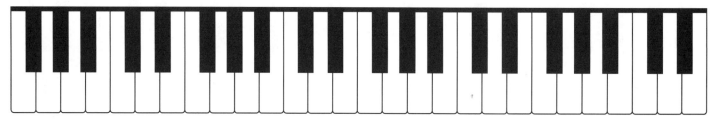

Practice Directions

Follow the practice directions on page 24 as you play "The A Song." Use left hand finger 3 (Tall Man) to play each A.

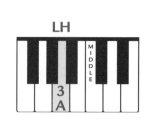

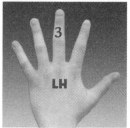

The A Song

Book 1
Track 14 (58)

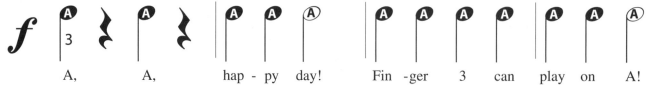

A,   A,   hap - py day!   Fin -ger   3   can   play   on   A!

ACTIVITY:
Finding A and B on the Keyboard

1. Color the HIGHEST A **green.**
2. Color the LOWEST A **purple.**
3. Color the other A's **brown.**

4. Color the HIGHEST B **red.**
5. Color the LOWEST B **yellow.**
6. Color the other B's **blue.**

ACTIVITY:
White Key Review: C, D, E

1. Color each C **yellow.**
2. Color each D **brown.**
3. Color each E **purple.**

Whole Rest

Introducing the Whole Rest

▬

A *whole rest* gets **four** counts. Rest for the whole measure.

▬

Count: Rest – 2 – 3 – 4

Practice Directions

Follow the practice directions on page 28 as you play "Little Dance" and "Rainy Day." Remember to lift your hand for the whole rests.

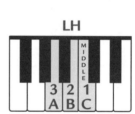

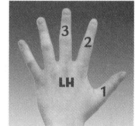

Little Dance
Book 1
Track 15 (59)

Repeat Sign
Play again.

𝆑 Ⓒ 1 Ⓑ 2 Ⓐ 3 ▬ Ⓒ 1 Ⓑ 2 Ⓐ 3 ▬

Count: 1   1   1 - 2   Rest - 2 - 3 - 4   1   1   1 - 2   Rest - 2 - 3 - 4
        Walk and stop.   Walk and stop.

Rainy Day
Book 1
Track 16 (60)

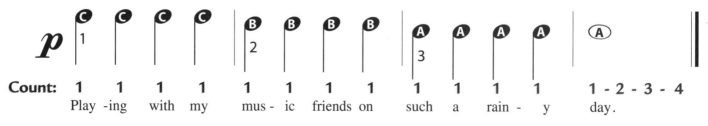

𝆏 Ⓒ 1 Ⓒ Ⓒ Ⓒ Ⓑ 2 Ⓑ Ⓑ Ⓑ Ⓐ 3 Ⓐ Ⓐ Ⓐ Ⓐ

Count: 1   1   1   1   1   1   1   1   1   1   1   1   1 - 2 - 3 - 4
       Play -ing with my mus - ic friends on such a rain - y   day.

34

ACTIVITY: The Whole Rest

A *whole rest* gets four counts.
Do not play for the entire measure.

How to Draw Whole Rests

Step 1: Trace the boxes hanging from short line.

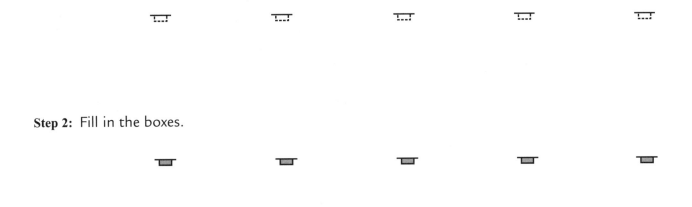

Step 2: Fill in the boxes.

Step 3: Draw four more whole rests.

Note Review

Draw the following notes:

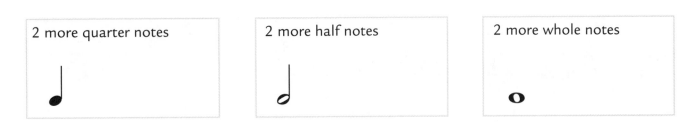

2 more quarter notes	2 more half notes	2 more whole notes

Finding F on the Keyboard

F is to the left of a three-black-key group.

Find each F on the keyboard below and color it pink.

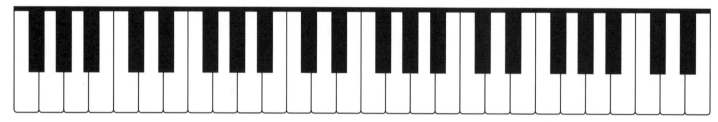

Practice Directions

Follow the practice directions on page 24 as you play "The F Song." Use right hand finger 4 (Ring Man) to play each F.

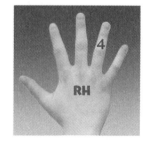

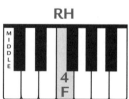

The F Song

Book 1
Track 17 (61)

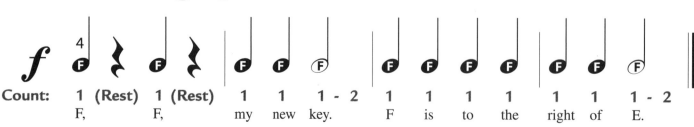

Count:	1	(Rest)	1	(Rest)	1	1	1 - 2	1	1	1	1	1	1	1 - 2
	F,		F,		my	new	key.	F	is	to	the	right	of	E.

Finding G on the Keyboard

G is the white key between F and A.

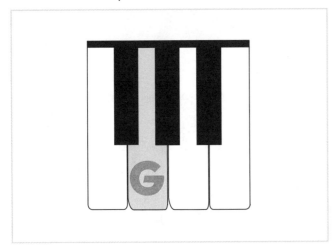

Find each G on the keyboard below and color it orange.

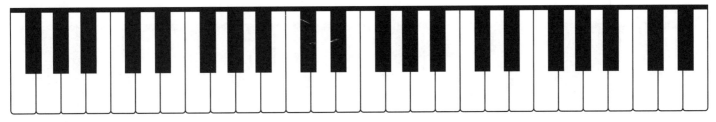

Practice Directions

Follow the practice directions on page 24 as you play "The G Song." Use right hand finger 5 (Pinky) to play each G.

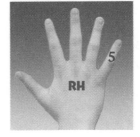

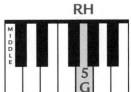

The G Song

Book 1
Track 18 (62)

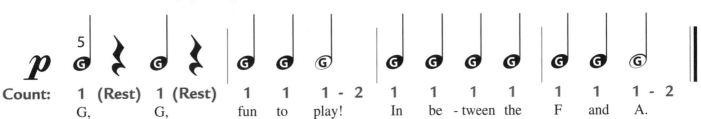

Count:	1 (Rest)	1 (Rest)	1	1	1 - 2	1	1	1	1	1	1	1 - 2
	G,	G,	fun	to	play!	In	be - tween	the		F	and	A.

ACTIVITY:
Finding F and G on the Keyboard

1. Color the HIGHEST F **pink.**
2. Color the LOWEST F **orange.**
3. Color the other F's **green.**

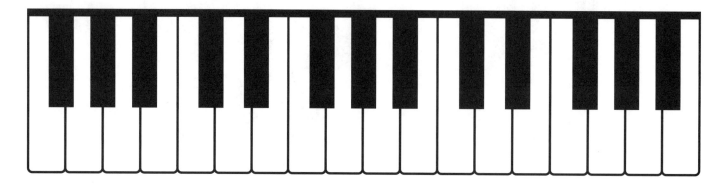

4. Color the HIGHEST G **red.**
5. Color the LOWEST G **yellow.**
6. Color the other G's **blue.**

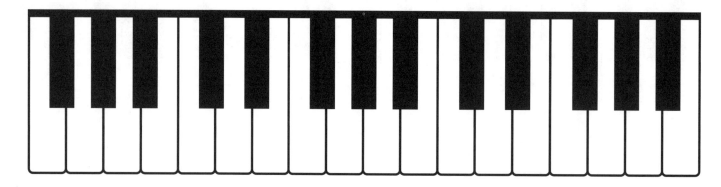

ACTIVITY:
White Key Review: F, G, A, B

1. Color each F **green.**
2. Color each G **red.**
3. Color each A **blue.**
4. Color each B **purple.**

$\frac{4}{4}$ Time Signature

You know how many beats are in each measure by looking at the *time signature*, which is always at the beginning of the music.

$\frac{4}{4}$ means **four** beats to each measure.

$\frac{4}{4}$ means a **quarter note** ♩ gets one beat.

Practice Directions
Follow the practice directions on page 28 as you play "Ice Cream" and "Music Stars!"

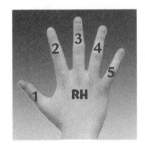

Middle C Position (RH)

Ice Cream

Book 1
 Track 19 (63)

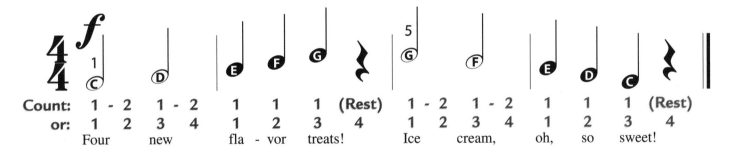

Count:	1 - 2	1 - 2	1	1	1	(Rest)	1 - 2	1 - 2	1	1	1	(Rest)
or:	1	2	3	4	1	2	3	4	1	2	3	4
	Four	new	fla -	vor	treats!		Ice	cream,	oh,	so	sweet!	

Music Stars!

Book 1
 Track 20 (64)

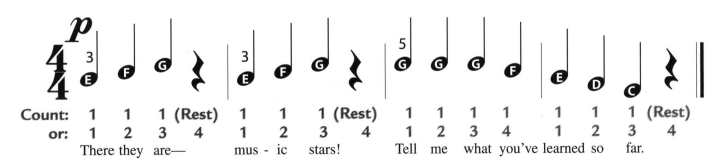

Count:	1	1	1	(Rest)	1	1	1	(Rest)	1	1	1	1	1	1	1	(Rest)
or:	1	2	3	4	1	2	3	4	1	2	3	4	1	2	3	4
	There	they	are—		mus -	ic	stars!		Tell	me	what	you've	learned	so	far.	

ACTIVITY:
The $\frac{4}{4}$ Time Signature

A $\frac{4}{4}$ time signature means there are four equal beats in every measure.

How to Draw the $\frac{4}{4}$ Time Signature

Step 1: Trace the number "4."   4   4   4   4

Step 2: Trace the second "4" below the first one. $\frac{4}{4}$ $\frac{4}{4}$ $\frac{4}{4}$ $\frac{4}{4}$

Draw four more $\frac{4}{4}$ time signatures. $\frac{4}{4}$

Note Review

Complete each measure by drawing the correct note (♩, 𝅗𝅥, or 𝅝) in the measure. Each measure should have four beats.

40

Time & Dotted Half Notes

Introducing the Dotted Half Note

A *dotted half note* gets **three** counts. It looks like a half note with a dot to the right of the notehead.

Count: 1 - 2 - 3

3 means **three** beats to each measure.

4 means a **quarter note** gets one beat.

Practice Directions
Follow the practice directions on page 28 as you play the songs on this page.

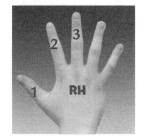

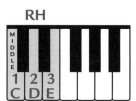
RH

Ready to Play

Book 1
Track 21 (65)

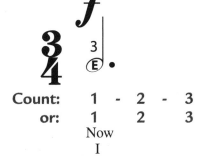

Count:	1	-	2	-	3	1	-	2	-	3	1	1	1	1	-	2	-	3
or:	1		2		3	1		2		3	1	2	3	1		2		3
	Now					it's					my	les	son	day.				
	I					am					read	dy	to	play.				

Middle C Position (LH)

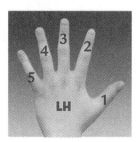

Play 3/4 Time

Book 1
Track 22 (66)

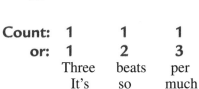

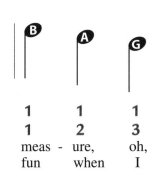

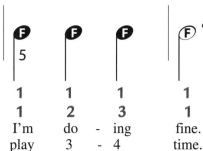

Count:	1	1	1	1	1	1	1	1	1	1	-	2	-	3
or:	1	2	3	1	2	3	1	2	3	1		2		3
	Three	beats	per	meas	ure,	oh,	I'm	do	ing	fine.				
	It's	so	much	fun	when	I	play	3	4	time.				

41

ACTIVITY: The Dotted Half Note

The *dotted half note* gets three counts.

How to Draw the Dotted Half Note

Step 1: Trace the half notes.

Step 2: Trace the dot to the right of each notehead.

Draw three more dotted half notes with stems going up and three dotted half notes with stems going down.

ACTIVITY: The $\frac{3}{4}$ Time Signature

A $\frac{3}{4}$ time signature means there are three equal beats in every measure.

How to Draw the $\frac{3}{4}$ Time Signature

Step 1: Trace the number "3."

3 3 3 3

Step 2: Trace the number "4" below the number 3.

Draw four more $\frac{3}{4}$ time signatures.

Moderately Loud Sounds

mf

The sign *mf* stands for ***mezzo forte***, which means to play **moderately loud**.

Practice Directions

Follow the practice directions on page 28 as you play "Yankee Doodle."

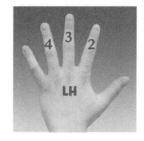
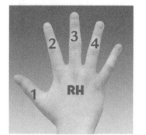

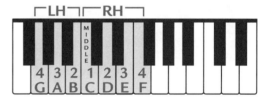

Yankee Doodle

Book 1
Track 23 (67)

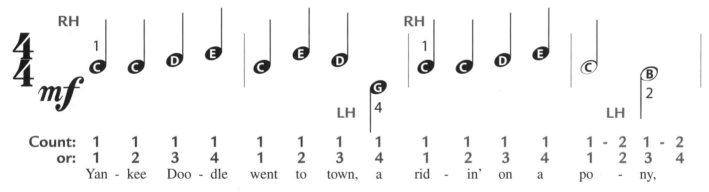

Count:	1	1	1	1	1	1	1	1	1	1	1	1	1 - 2	1 - 2
or:	1	2	3	4	1	2	3	4	1	2	3	4	1 2	3 4
	Yan -	kee	Doo -	dle	went	to	town,	a	rid -	in'	on	a	po -	ny,

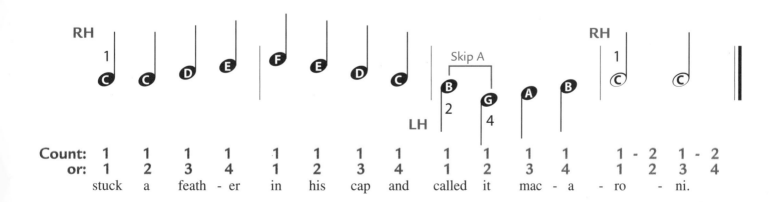

Count:	1	1	1	1	1	1	1	1	1	1	1	1	1 - 2	1 - 2
or:	1	2	3	4	1	2	3	4	1	2	3	4	1 2	3 4
	stuck	a	feath -	er	in	his	cap	and	called	it	mac -	a -	ro -	ni.

ACTIVITY: Review

Draw a line connecting the dots to match the symbol to its name.

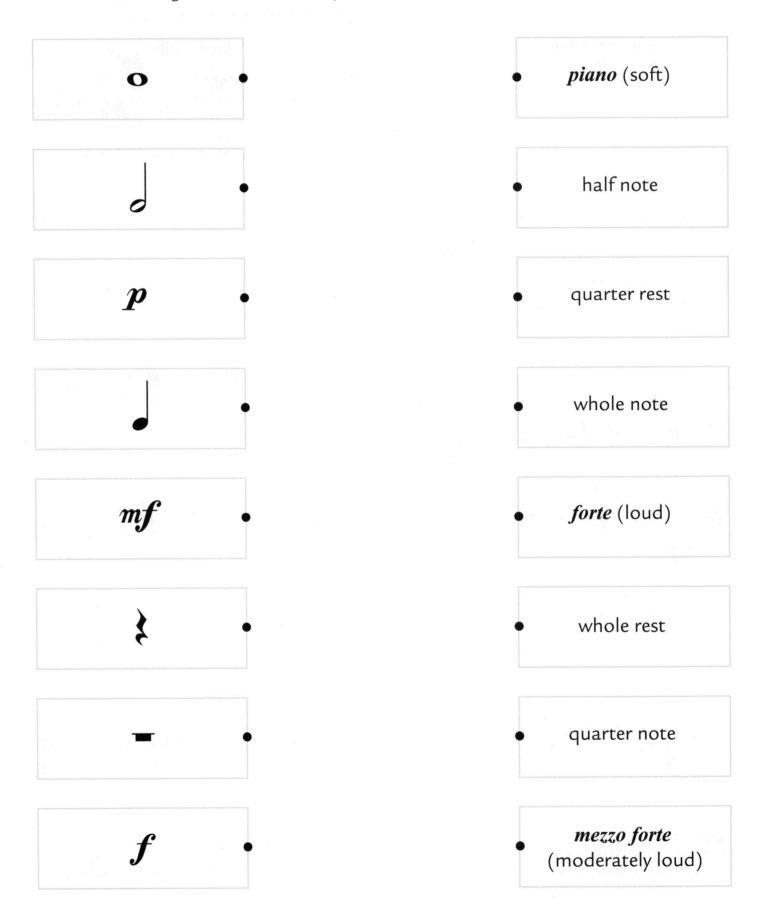

o   •   •   *piano* (soft)

  •   •   half note

p   •   •   quarter rest

  •   •   whole note

mf   •   •   *forte* (loud)

  •   •   whole rest

  •   •   quarter note

f   •   •   *mezzo forte* (moderately loud)

The Staff

Each note has a name. That name depends on where the note is found on the *staff*.
The staff is made up of five horizontal lines and the spaces between those lines.

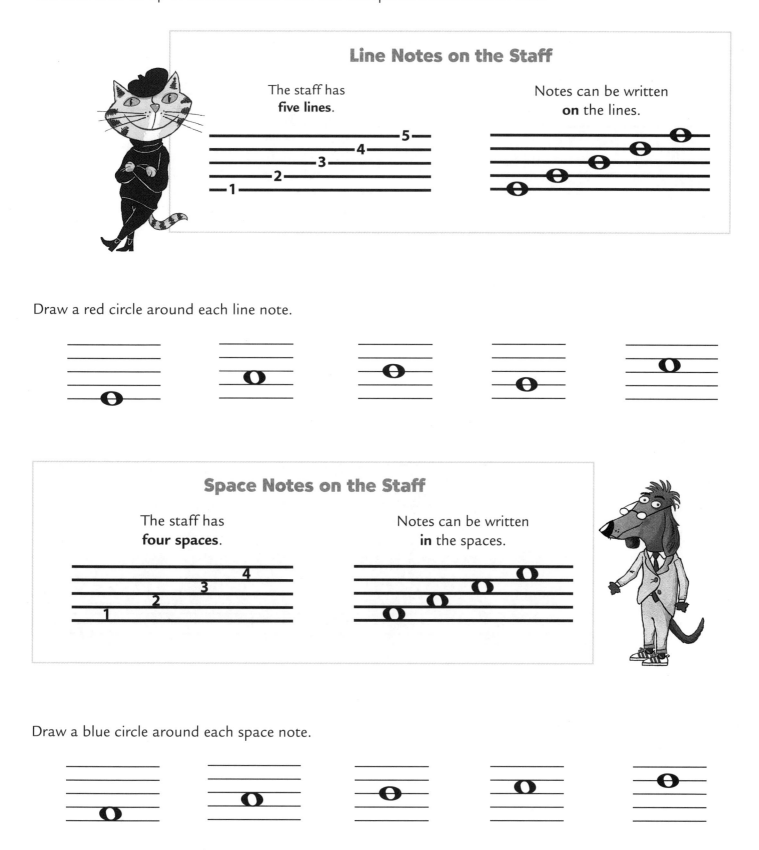

Line Notes on the Staff

The staff has **five lines**.

Notes can be written **on** the lines.

Draw a red circle around each line note.

Space Notes on the Staff

The staff has **four spaces**.

Notes can be written **in** the spaces.

Draw a blue circle around each space note.

ACTIVITY: The Staff

Music is written on a STAFF of 5 lines and 4 spaces.

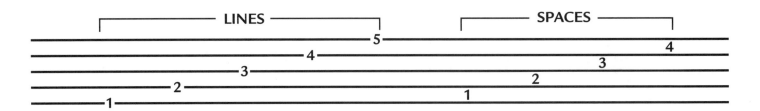

Some notes are written on LINES.

Some notes are written in SPACES.

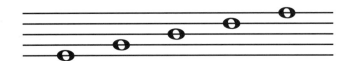

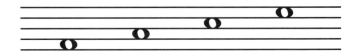

1. Circle each LINE NOTE.

2. Circle each SPACE NOTE.

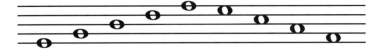

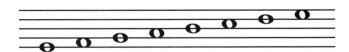

3. Name the line for each note in the box below the staff.

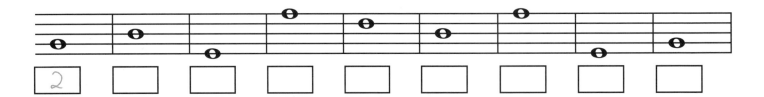

4. Name the space for each note in the box below the staff.

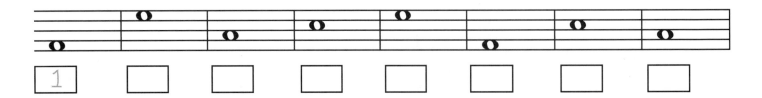

Treble Clef

As music notation progressed through history, the staff had 2 to 20 lines. Symbols were invented that would always give a reference point for all other notes. These symbols are called *clefs*.

Introducing the Treble Clef

Play *treble clef* notes with the right hand.

Treble Clef Middle C

Middle C is the C nearest the middle of the piano keyboard.

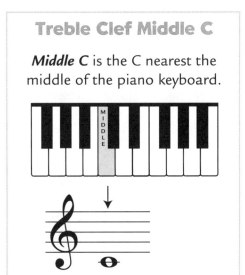

Trace the treble clef with a black crayon, and trace the middle C with a green crayon.

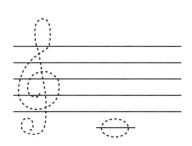

Steps

From one white key to the next, up or down, is a *step*.

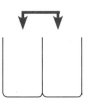

Steps are written **line to space** or **space to line**.

Treble Clef D

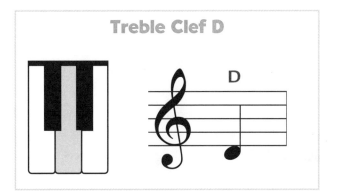

D

Practice Directions

Follow the practice directions on page 28 as you play "Take a Step." This song uses repeated notes and steps up and down.

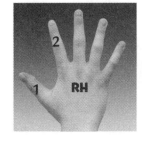 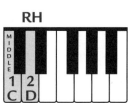

RH

Book 1
Track 24 (68)

Take a Step

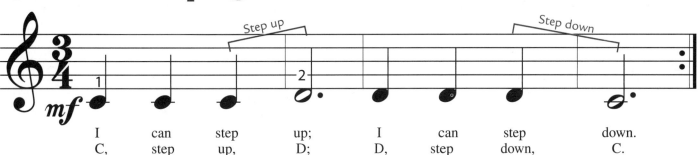

Step up   Step down

mf

I   can   step   up;   I   can   step   down.
C,   step   up,   D;   D,   step   down,   C.

47

Treble Clef E

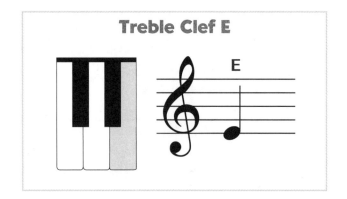

Practice Directions

Follow the practice directions on page 28 as you play the songs on this page.

Circle the repeated notes in "Stepping Fun."
All other notes are steps.

Stepping Fun

Book 1
Track 25 (69)

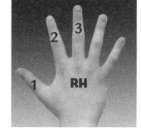

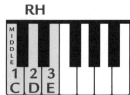
RH

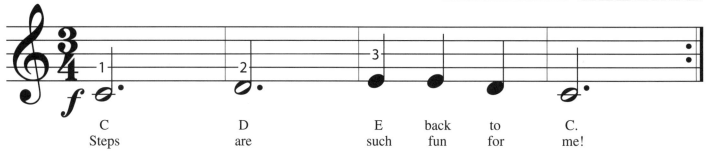

| C | D | E | back | to | C. |
| Steps | are | such | fun | for | me! |

Treble Clef F

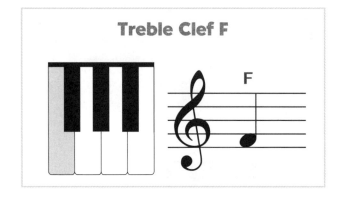

Treble Clef G

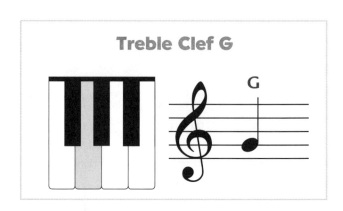

This song uses all five fingers of the right hand.

Right Hand Song

Book 1
Track 26 (70)

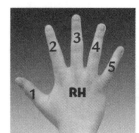

RH

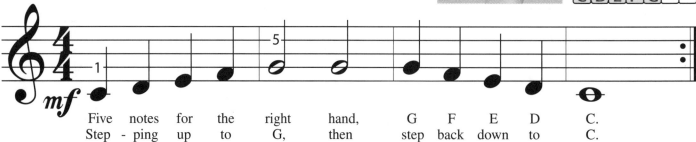

| Five | notes | for | the | right | hand, | G | F | E | D | C. |
| Step - | ping | up | to | G, | then | step | back | down | to | C. |

48

ACTIVITY: The Treble Clef

The TREBLE CLEF SIGN 𝄞 locates the G above the middle of the keyboard.

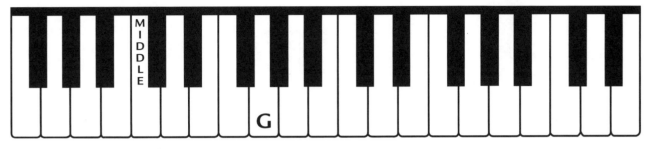

This is the G line. 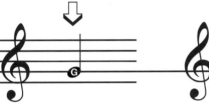 The clef sign curls around the G line.

By moving up or down from the G line, you can name any note on the treble staff.

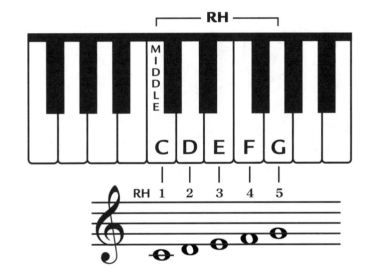

1. Write the name of each note in the square below it. Then play and say the note names.

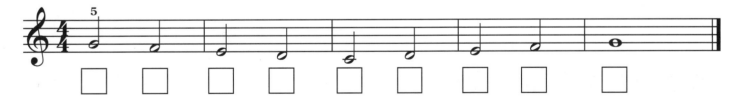

2. Write the name of each note in the square below it. The letters in each group of squares will spell a familiar word.

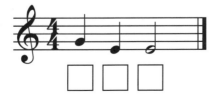  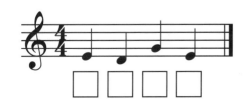

Bass Clef

Introducing the Bass Clef

Play **bass clef** notes with the left hand.

Bass Clef

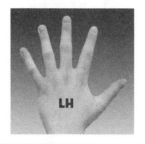

LH

Bass Clef Middle C

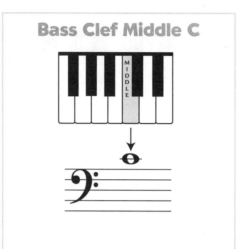

Trace the bass clef with a black crayon, and trace the middle C with a green crayon.

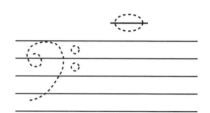

Bass Clef B

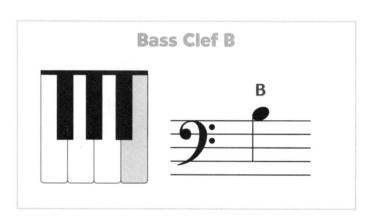

B

Practice Directions

Follow the practice directions on page 28 as you play "Stepping Down." Measures 2 and 4 of this song use repeated notes.

Book 1
Track 27 (71)

Stepping Down

LH
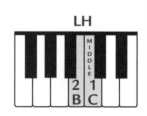
2 B 1 C

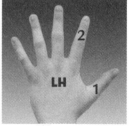
2
LH
1

Step - ping down from mid - dle C,   C,   B,   look   at   me!
There's so   much that   I   can   do.   Step down,   so   can   you.

50

Bass Clef A

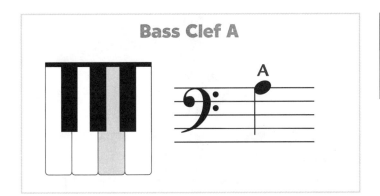

Practice Directions

Follow the practice directions on page 28 as you play the songs on this page.

Circle the repeated notes in "Music to Share." All other notes are steps.

Music to Share

Book 1
Track 28 (72)

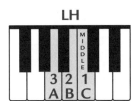

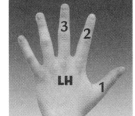

p

Could		we		go	down	the	stairs?
We		have		mu -	sic	to	share.

Bass Clef G

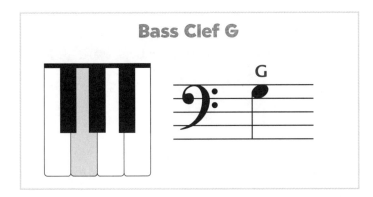

Bass Clef F

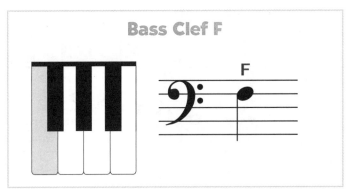

This song uses all five fingers of the left hand.

Left Hand Song

Book 1
Track 29 (73)

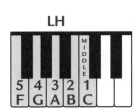

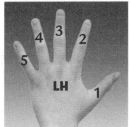

f

Five	notes	for	the	left	hand,	F,	G,	A,	B,	C.
Step	-ping	down	to	F,	then	step	back	up	to	C.

ACTIVITY: The Bass Clef

The BASS CLEF SIGN 𝄢 locates the F below the middle of the keyboard.

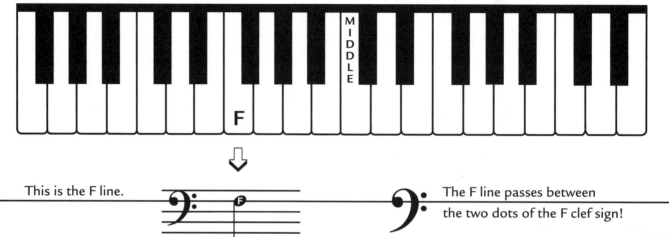

This is the F line. 𝄢 F

The F line passes between the two dots of the F clef sign!

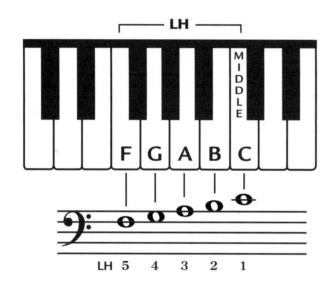

By moving up or down from the F line, you can name any note on the bass staff.

LH 5   4   3   2   1

1. Write the name of each note in the square below it. Then play and say the note names.

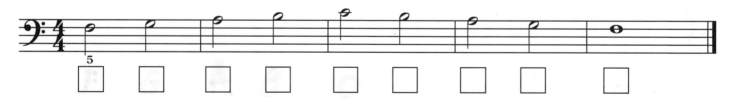

5

□ □ □ □ □ □ □ □ □

2. Write the name of each note in the square below it. The letters in each group of squares will spell a familiar word.

□ □ □   □ □ □   □ □ □

52

Skips

When you skip over a white key, you also skip a finger.

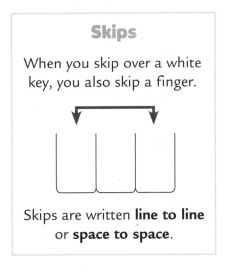

Skips are written **line to line** or **space to space**.

Practice Directions

Follow the practice directions on page 28 as you play the songs on this page.

Measure 3 of "Music Friend" uses repeated notes.

Music Friend

Book 1
Track 30 (74)

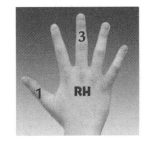
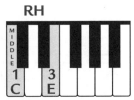

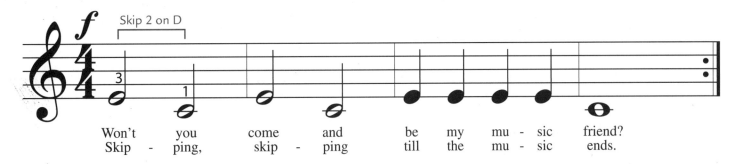

Won't you come and be my mu - sic friend?
Skip - ping, skip - ping till the mu - sic ends.

Find and circle the two steps in "Circle Time."

Circle Time

Book 1
Track 31 (75)

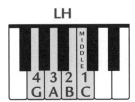
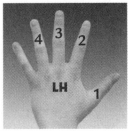

Cir - cling skips can sure be fun! In this piece there's more than one.
Grab a cray - on, skip to B. Find - ing skips is fun for me!

ACTIVITY:
Skips

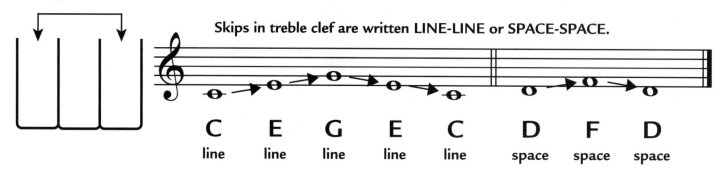

Skips in treble clef are written LINE-LINE or SPACE-SPACE.

C	E	G	E	C	D	F	D
line	line	line	line	line	space	space	space

1. Circle each skip in treble clef.

Skips in bass clef are also written LINE-LINE or SPACE-SPACE.

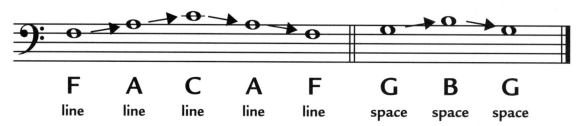

F	A	C	A	F	G	B	G
line	line	line	line	line	space	space	space

2. Circle each skip in bass clef.

The Grand Staff

When the treble staff and bass staff are joined together with a **brace**, it is called the **grand staff**. The grand staff is used to show notes for both the right and left hands. A short line between the two staffs is used for **middle C**.

Middle C Position on the Grand Staff

When playing in middle C position, either thumb can play middle C.

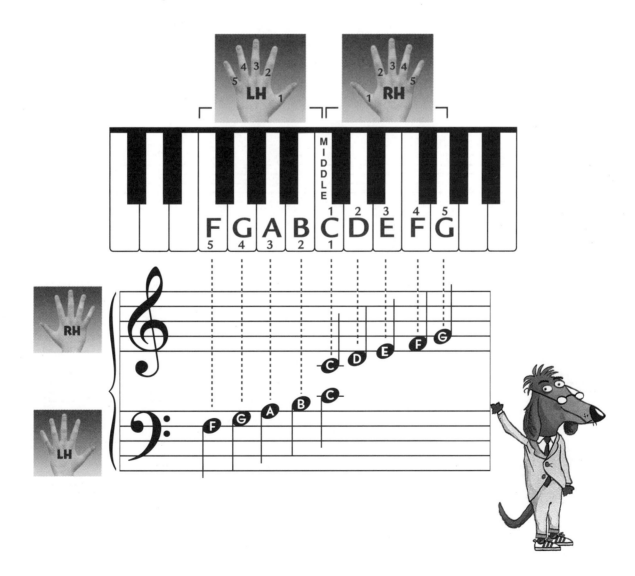

ACTIVITY: The Grand Staff

The TREBLE STAFF and the BASS STAFF are joined together
with a BRACE and a BAR LINE to make a GRAND STAFF.

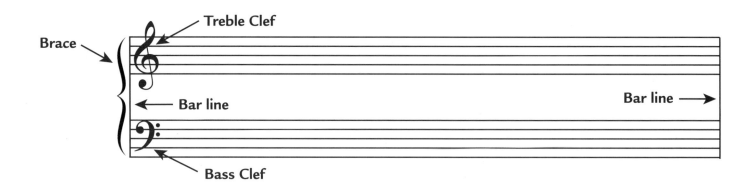

Draw two grand staffs by following these steps:
1. Draw a TREBLE CLEF sign on the top staff.
2. Draw a BASS CLEF sign on the staff just below it.
3. Draw a BAR LINE at the beginning and end of the two staffs.
4. Draw a BRACE at the beginning of the two staffs.

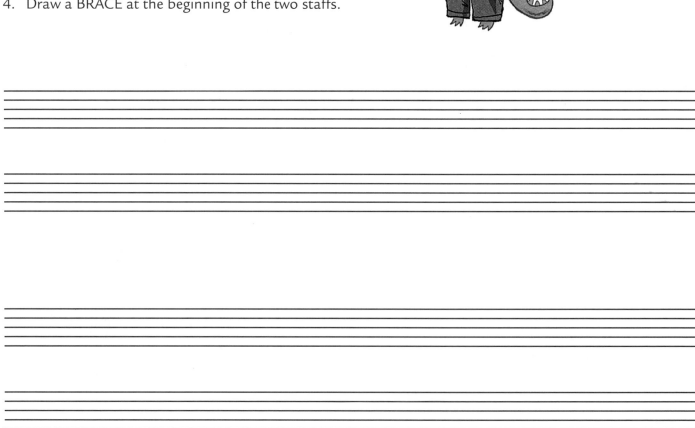

Practice Directions

Follow the practice directions on page 28 as you play "Just for You."

Both hands of "Just for You" play steps, skips, and repeated notes.

Middle C Position

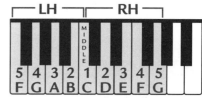

Just for You

Book 1
 Track 32 (76)

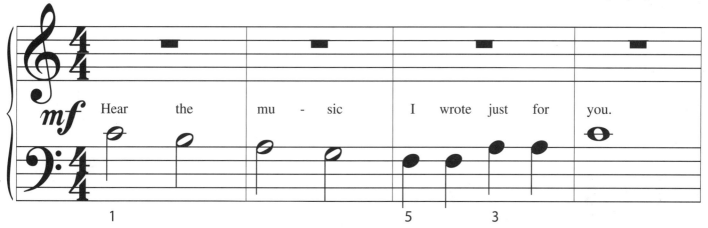

Hear the mu - sic   I wrote just for you.

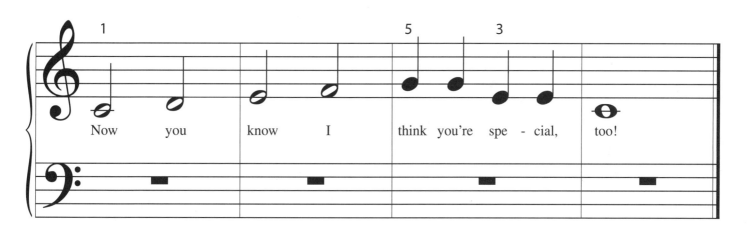

Now you know I   think you're spe - cial, too!

Half Rest

Introducing the Half Rest

![half rest symbol]

A *half rest*
gets **two** counts. Do not
play for two counts, which is
the same as two quarter notes.

Count: Rest – 2
Or: 1   2

Practice Directions
Follow the practice directions on page 28
as you play "Haydn's Symphony."

Book 1
Track 33 (77)

Haydn's Symphony

Middle C Position

Franz Joseph Haydn

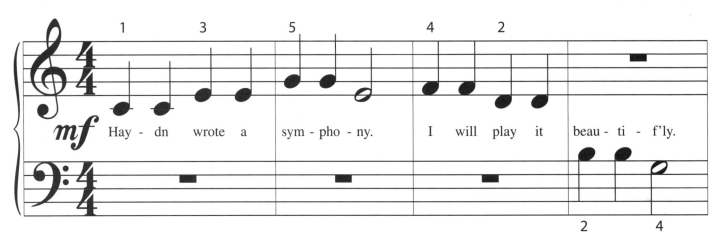

Hay - dn wrote a sym - pho - ny. I will play it beau - ti - f'ly.

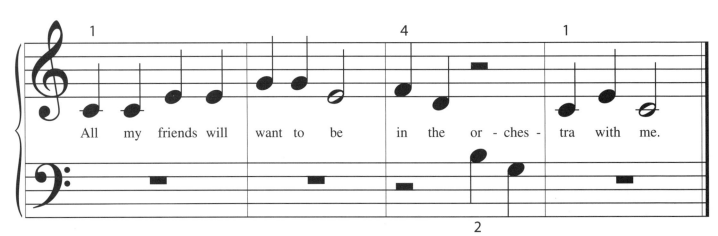

All my friends will want to be in the or - ches - tra with me.

ACTIVITY: The Half Rest

A *half rest* means to be silent for two counts.

How to Draw Half Rests

Step 1: Trace the box on top of the middle line of the staff.

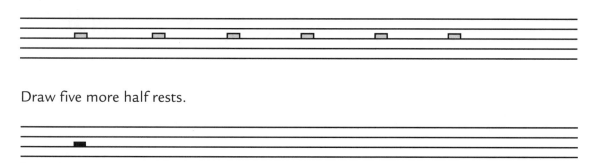

Step 2: Fill in the box.

Draw five more half rests.

Note and Rest Review

Draw a line connecting the dots to match the note with the rest that gets the same number of counts.

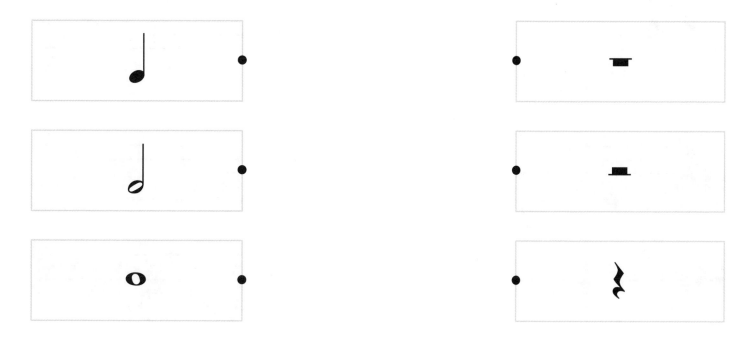

London Bridge

Middle C Position

Book 1
Track 34 (78)

Practice Directions
See page 28.

Notice that both hands begin with finger 2 for this song.

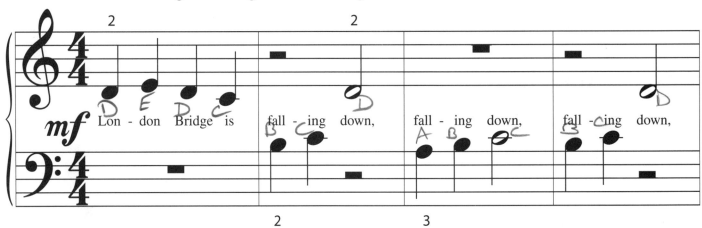

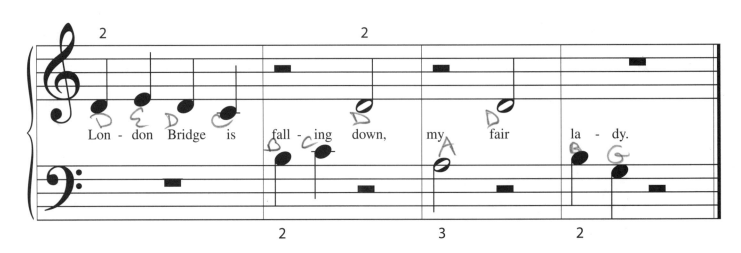

60

Twinkle, Twinkle, Little Star

Middle C Position

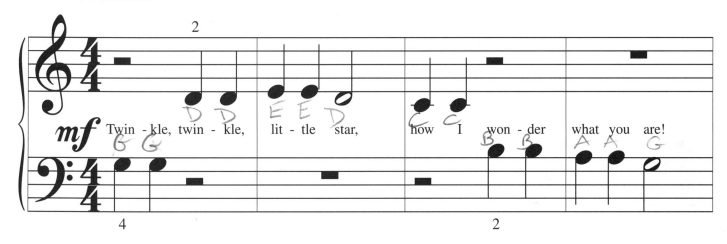

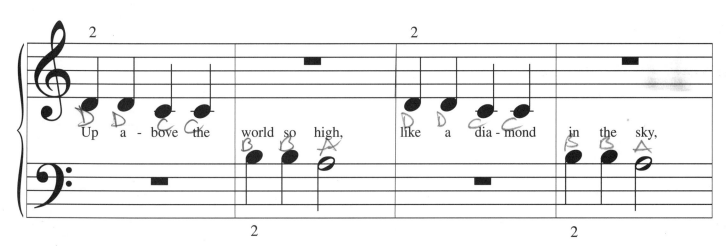

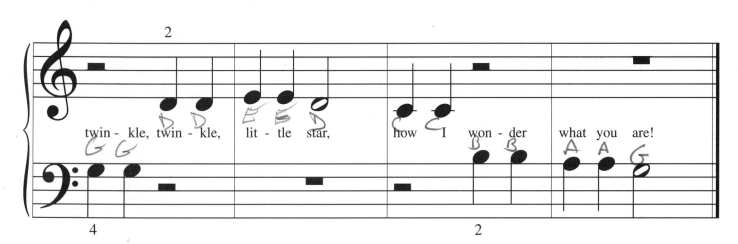

61

ACTIVITY: Middle C Position for LH

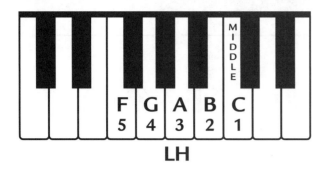

1. Write the names of the keys in the LH MIDDLE C POSITION on the keyboard.

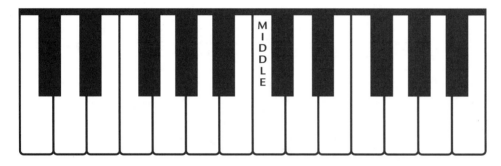

2. Draw lines connecting the dots to match the LH finger number with the key that it plays in MIDDLE C POSITION.

LH 5

LH 4

LH 3

LH 2

LH 1

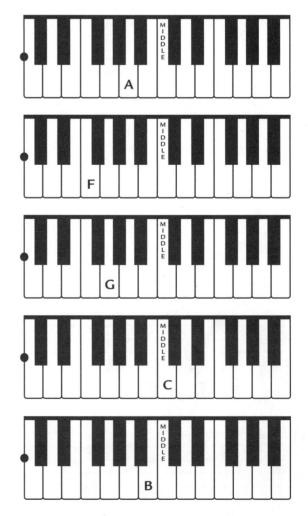

Jingle Bells

Middle C Position

Book 1
Track 36 (80)

James S. Pierpont

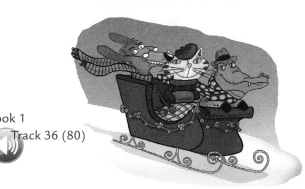

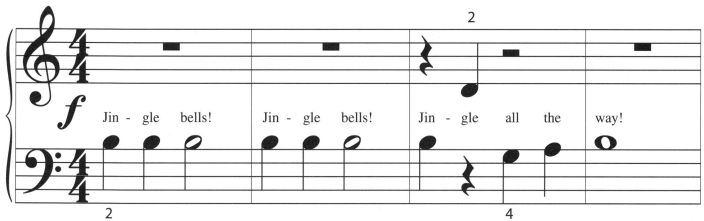

Jin - gle bells! Jin - gle bells! Jin - gle all the way!

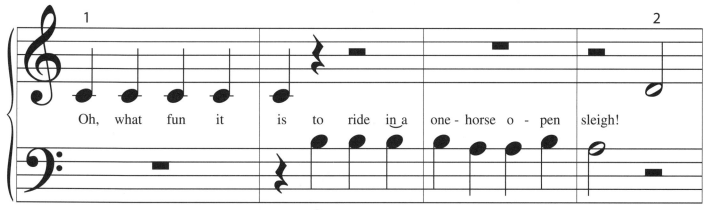

Oh, what fun it is to ride in a one - horse o - pen sleigh!

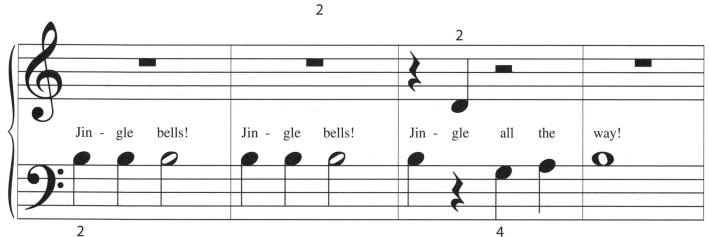

Jin - gle bells! Jin - gle bells! Jin - gle all the way!

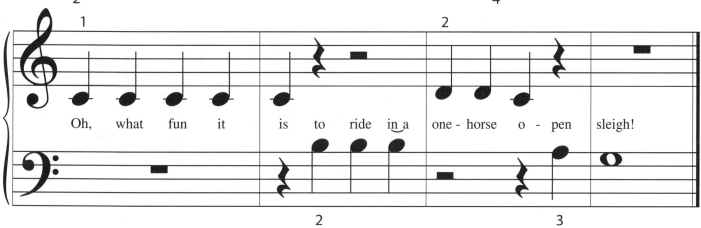

Oh, what fun it is to ride in a one - horse o - pen sleigh!

ACTIVITY: Middle C Position for RH

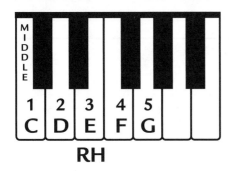

RH

1. Write the names of the keys in the RH MIDDLE C POSITION on the keyboard.

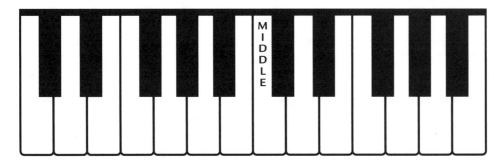

2. Draw lines connecting the dots to match the RH finger number with the key that it plays in MIDDLE C POSITION.

| RH 1 | ● |

| RH 2 | ● |

| RH 3 | ● |

| RH 4 | ● |

| RH 5 | ● |

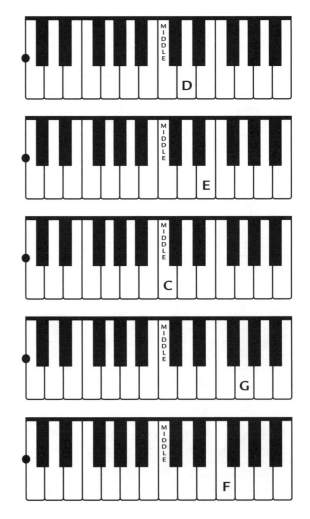

Bass Clef C

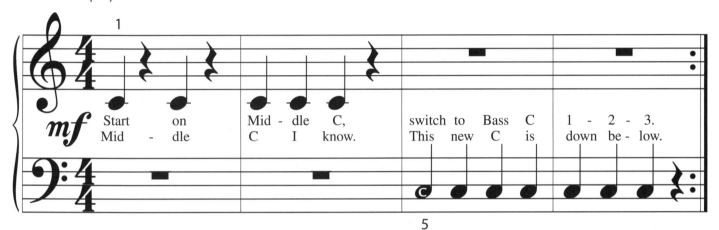

Practice Directions
See page 28.

New C

Book 1
Track 37 (81)

Both hands play C.

Start on Mid - dle C, switch to Bass C 1 - 2 - 3.
Mid - dle C I know. This new C is down be - low.

Bass Clef D

Three "D"-lightful Friends

Book 1
Track 38 (82)

Both hands play D.

Stand here next to me. Three "D"- light - ful friends are we!

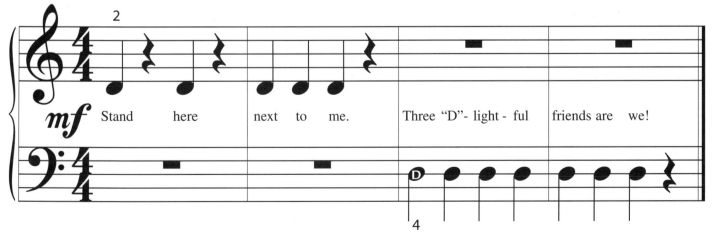

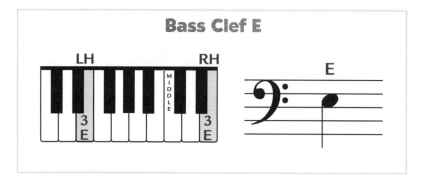

Finger 3 on E

Book 1
Track 39 (83)

Both hands play E.

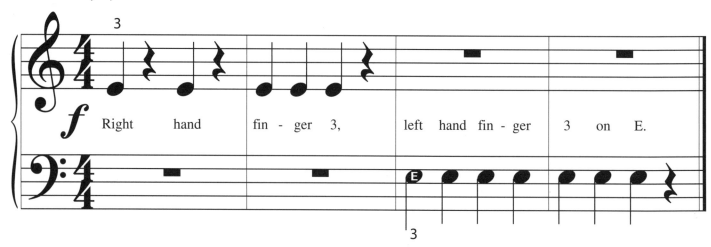

Right hand fin - ger 3, left hand fin - ger 3 on E.

Practice Directions
See page 28.

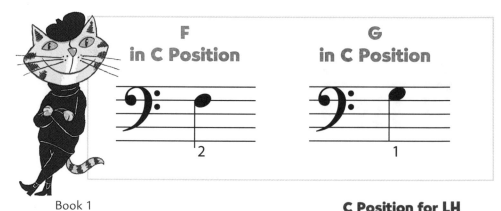

F in C Position

G in C Position

Great Big Day

Book 1
Track 40 (84)

C Position

This song uses all five fingers of the left hand.

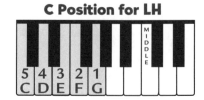

C Position for LH

5 4 3 2 1
C D E F G

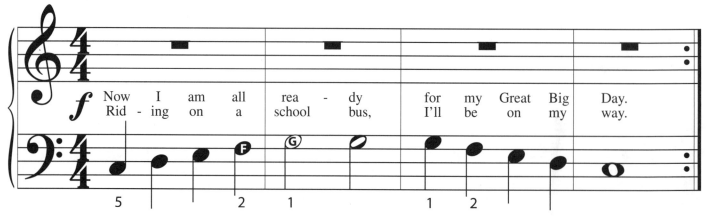

Now I am all rea - dy for my Great Big Day.
Rid - ing on a school bus, I'll be on my way.

ACTIVITY: C Position for LH

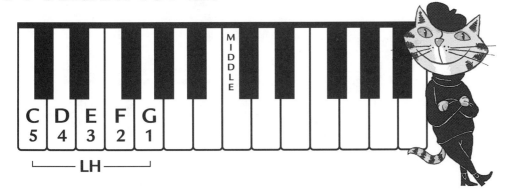

1. Write the names of the keys in the LH C POSITION on the keyboard.

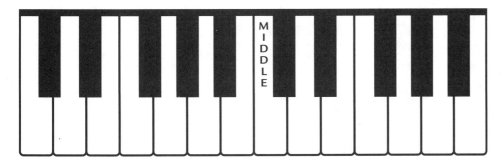

2. Draw lines connecting the dots to match the LH finger number with the key that it plays in C POSITION.

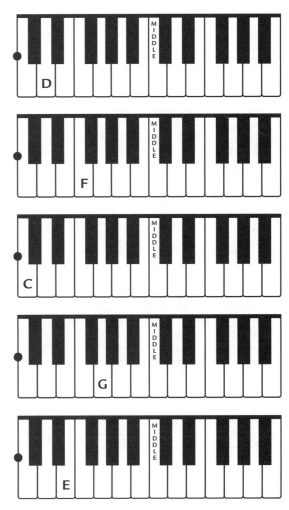

C Position on the Grand Staff

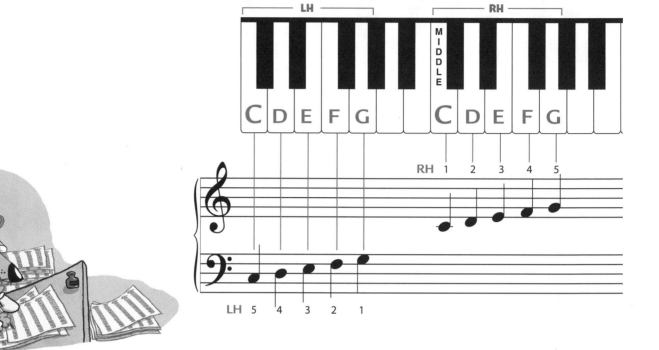

Ode to Joy

Book 1
Track 41 (85)

(Theme from the Ninth Symphony)

Practice Directions
See page 28.

Both hands begin with finger 3 on E.

Ludwig van Beethoven

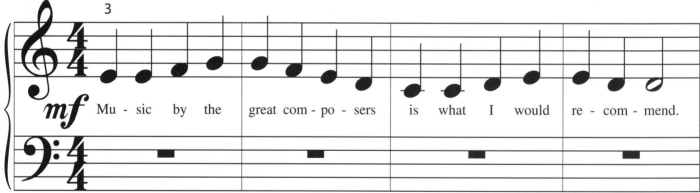

Mu - sic by the great com - po - sers is what I would re - com - mend.

When I play Bee - tho - ven's mu - sic I wish it would ne - ver end.

ACTIVITY:
C Position on the Grand Staff

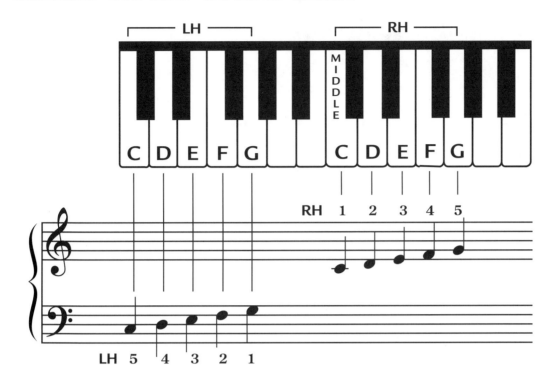

1. Circle each of the LH and RH notes from the C position on the Grand Staff.

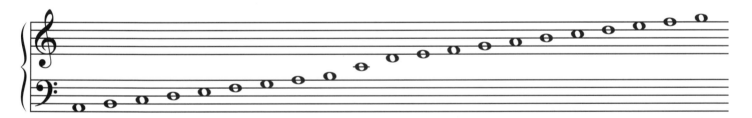

2. Write the name of each note in the square below it. Then play and say the note names.

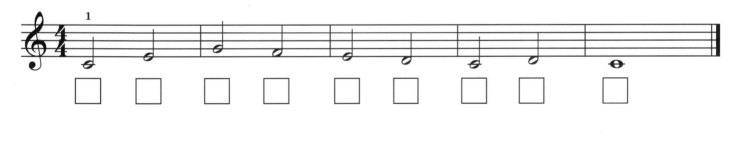

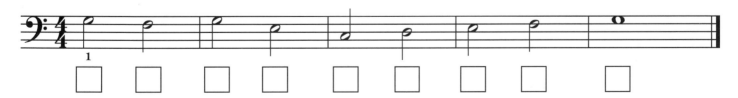

Row, Row, Row Your Boat

C Position

Book 1

Track 42 (86)

Practice Directions
See page 28.

A whole rest gets three beats in 3/4 time.

Row, row, row your boat,

gent – ly down the stream.

Mer – ri – ly, mer – ri – ly, mer – ri – ly, mer – ri – ly,

life is but a dream.

Hush, Little Baby

C Position

Book 1

Track 43 (87)

Each line begins with the left hand and changes to the right.

Practice Directions
See page 28.

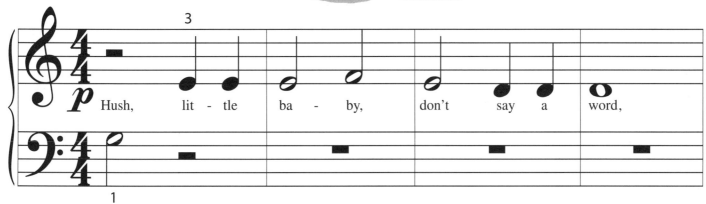

Hush, lit - tle ba - by, don't say a word,

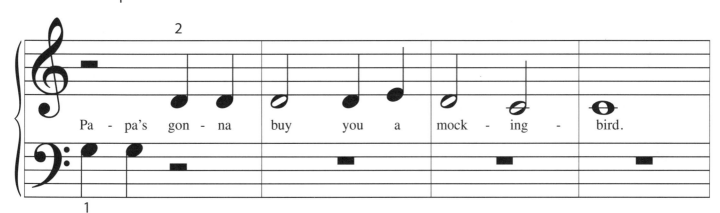

Pa - pa's gon - na buy you a mock - ing - bird.

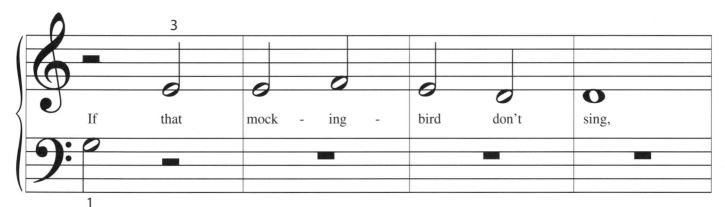

If that mock - ing - bird don't sing,

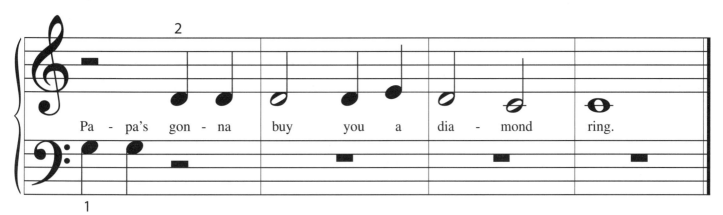

Pa - pa's gon - na buy you a dia - mond ring.

The Wheels on the Bus

Book 1
Track 44 (88)

C Position

Practice Directions
See page 28.

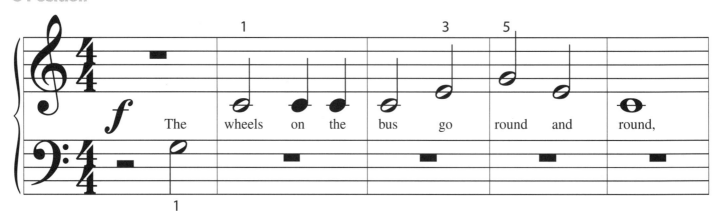

The wheels on the bus go round and round,

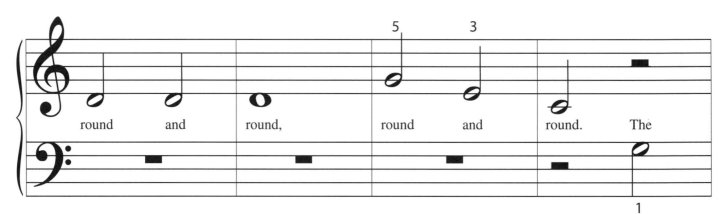

round and round, round and round. The

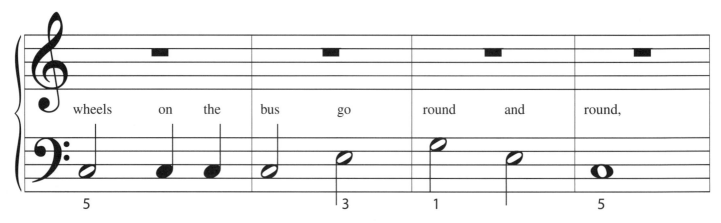

wheels on the bus go round and round,

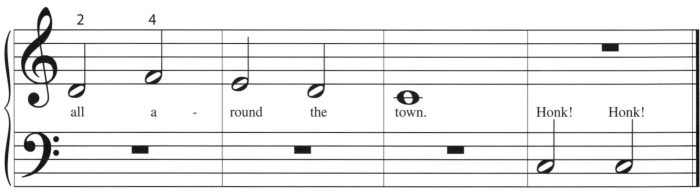

all a - round the town. Honk! Honk!

ACTIVITY:
Middle C Position on the Grand Staff

1. Print the letter names for both the LH and RH C POSITION on the keyboard.
2. Draw a line to connect each note on the staff to the appropriate key on the keyboard.

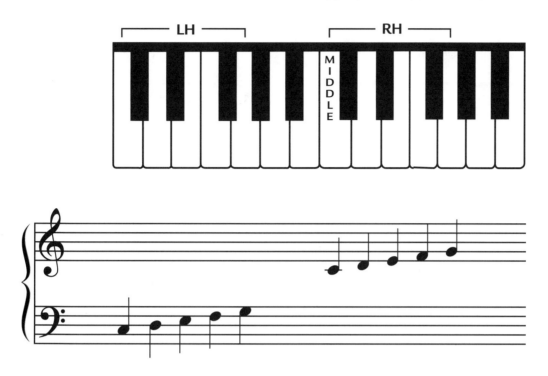

3. Draw lines connecting the dots on the matching boxes.

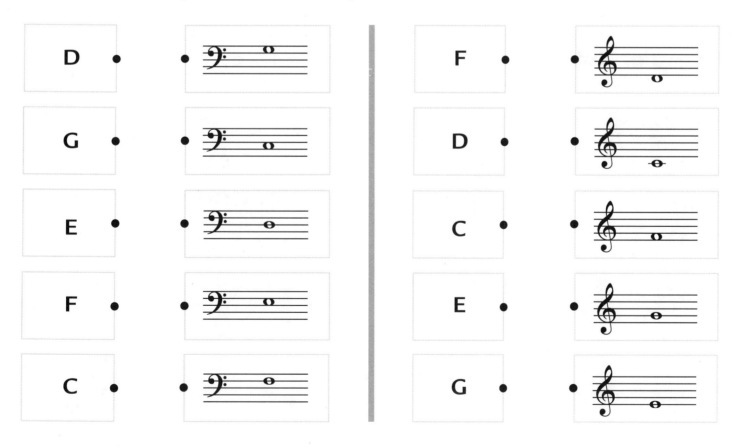

Music Matching Games

Symbols

Draw a line to match each symbol on the left to its name on the right.

1. ♩
2. 3/4
3. :‖
4. *mf*
5. ▬
6. 𝅝
7. 𝄽
8. *f*
9. 𝅗𝅥
10. *p*
11. 4/4
12. ▬
13. 𝅗𝅥.

- repeat sign
- moderately loud
- three beats in each measure
- quarter rest
- quarter note
- loud
- four beats in each measure
- dotted half note
- whole note
- half rest
- half note
- whole rest
- soft

Treble Clef Notes

Draw a line to match each treble clef note on the left to its correct letter name on the right.

1.
2.
3.
4.
5.

- C
- D
- E
- F
- G

Bass Clef Notes

Draw a line to match each bass clef note on the left to its correct letter name on the right.

1.
2.
3.
4.
5.
6.
7.

- C
- D
- E
- F
- G
- A
- B

Answer Key

Symbols
1. quarter note
2. three beats in each measure
3. repeat sign
4. moderately loud
5. half rest
6. whole note
7. quarter rest
8. loud
9. half note
10. soft
11. four beats in each measure
12. whole rest
13. dotted half note

Treble Clef Notes
1. G
2. D
3. C
4. E
5. F

Bass Clef Notes
1. D
2. G
3. C
4. B
5. A
6. F
7. E

Practice Directions

Follow these practice directions as you play the pieces throughout the book!

1. Clap (or tap) and count aloud evenly.

2. Point to the notes and count aloud evenly.

3. Say the finger numbers aloud while playing them in the air.

4. Play and say the finger numbers.

5. Play and say the note names.

6. Play and sing the words.

Middle C Position

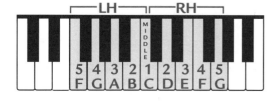

Camptown Races

Book 2
Track 1 (50)

Middle C Position

Stephen Foster
(1826–1864)

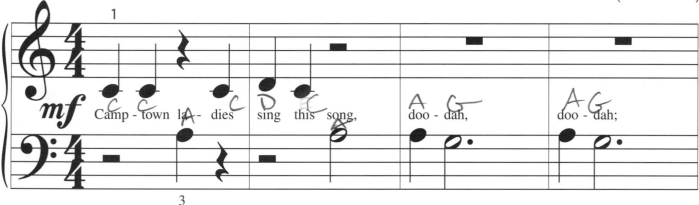

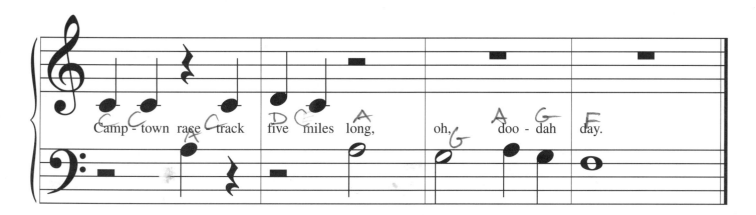

The Mulberry Bush

Book 2
Track 2 (51)

Middle C Position

Practice Directions
Follow the practice directions on page 75 as you play "The Mulberry Bush."

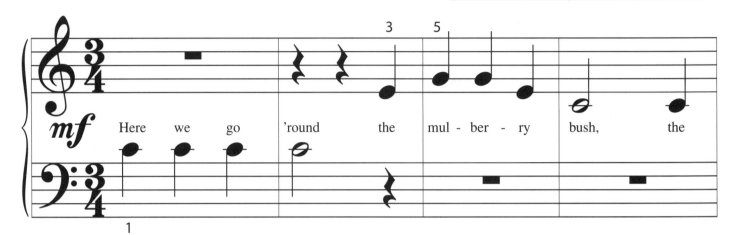

Here we go 'round the mul - ber - ry bush, the

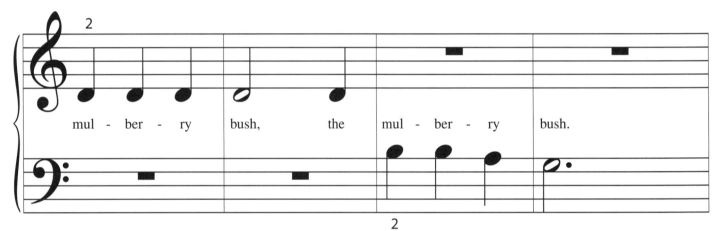

mul - ber - ry bush, the mul - ber - ry bush.

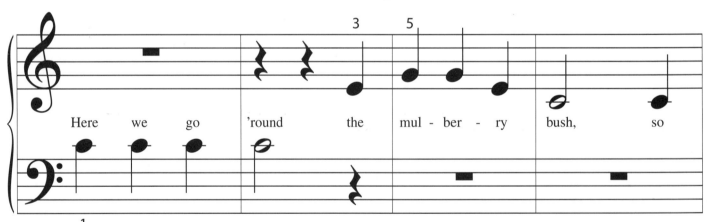

Here we go 'round the mul - ber - ry bush, so

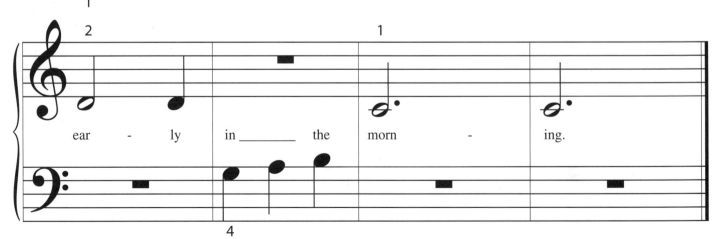

ear - ly in _____ the morn - ing.

ACTIVITY:
Middle C Position on the Grand Staff

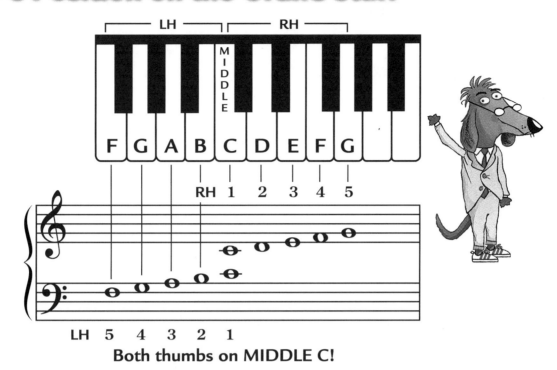

Both thumbs on MIDDLE C!

1. Using whole notes, draw the LH notes from the Middle C Position in the BASS staff under the squares.
2. Using whole notes, draw the RH notes from the Middle C Position in the TREBLE staff over the squares.

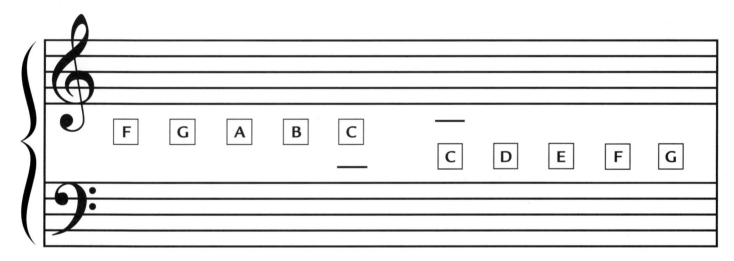

3. Write the name of each note in the square below it. Then play and say the note names.

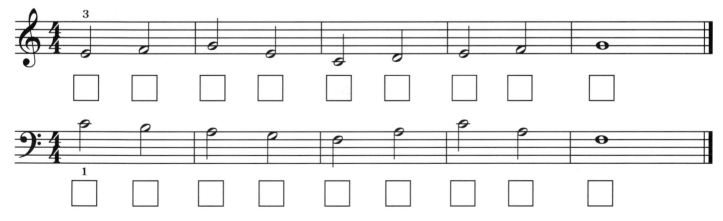

Jolly Old Saint Nicholas

Book 2
Track 3 (52)

Middle C Position

Practice Directions
Follow the practice directions on page 75.

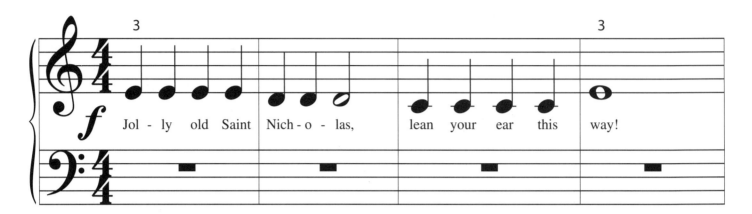

Jol - ly old Saint Nich - o - las, lean your ear this way!

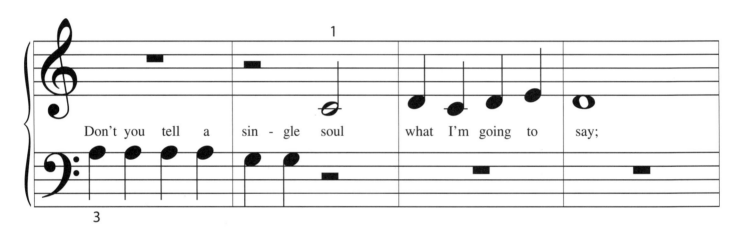

Don't you tell a sin - gle soul what I'm going to say;

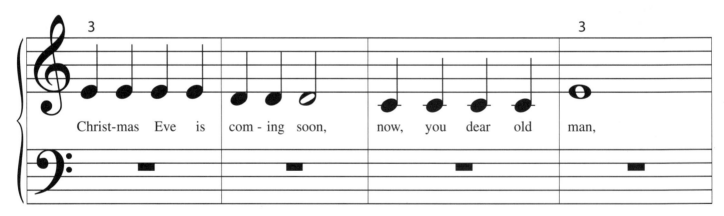

Christ-mas Eve is com - ing soon, now, you dear old man,

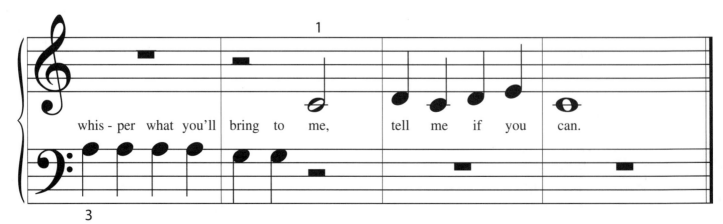

whis - per what you'll bring to me, tell me if you can.

Practice Directions
Follow the practice directions on page 75.

Theme from New World Symphony

Book 2
Track 4 (53)

Middle C Position
This famous melody is sometimes known as "Going Home."

Anton Dvořák
(1841–1904)

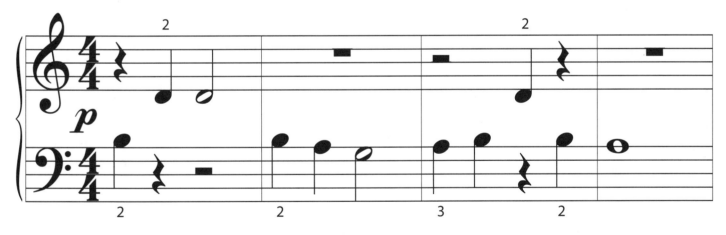

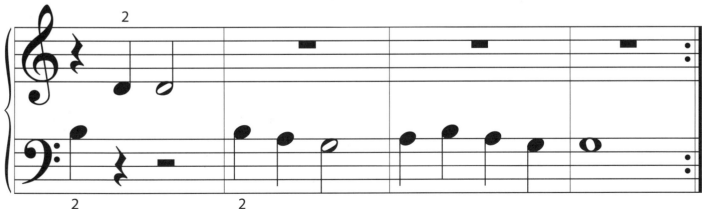

79

ACTIVITY:
Middle C Position on the Grand Staff

1. Print the letter names for both the LH and RH MIDDLE C POSITION on the keyboard below.

2. Draw a line to connect each note on the staff to the appropriate key on the keyboard.

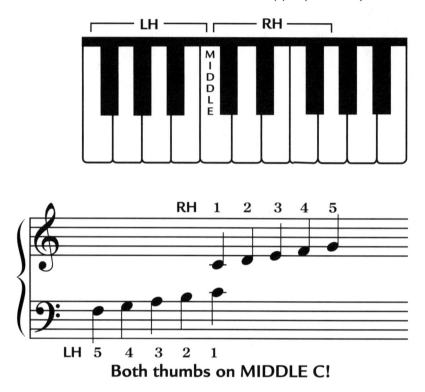

Both thumbs on MIDDLE C!

3. Draw lines connecting the dots on the matching boxes.

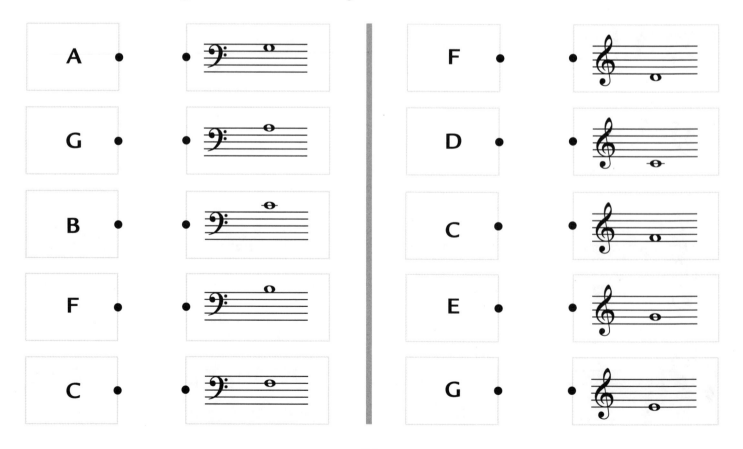

Practice Directions
Follow the practice directions on page 75.

C Position

Book 2
Track 5 (54)

Mary Had a Little Lamb
C Position

Mary had a lit-tle lamb, lit-tle lamb, lit-tle lamb.

Mary had a lit-tle lamb its fleece was white as snow.

God Is So Good

Book 2
Track 6 (55)

C Position

Practice Directions
Follow the practice directions on page 75.

God is so good, God is so good,

God is so good, He's so good to me!

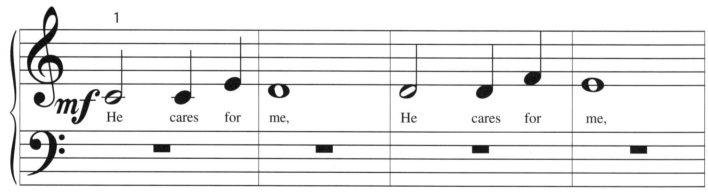

He cares for me, He cares for me,

He cares for me, He's so good to me!

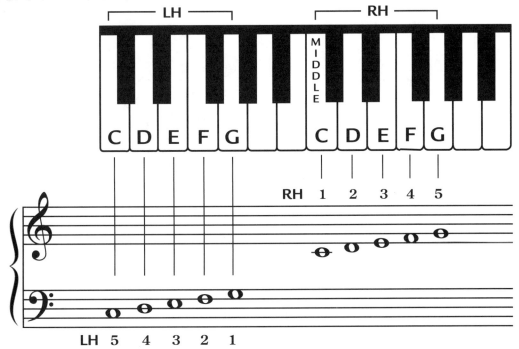

1. Using whole notes, draw the LH notes from C Position in the BASS staff under the squares.

2. Using whole notes, draw the RH notes from C Position in the TREBLE staff over the squares.

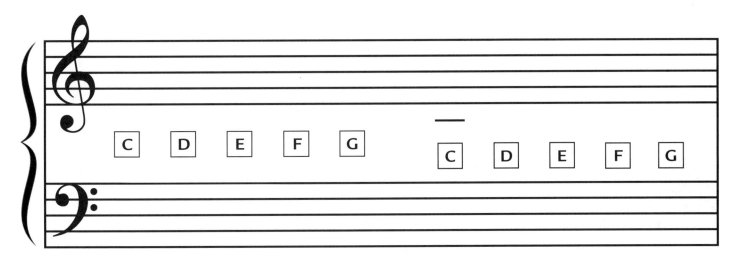

3. Write the name of each note in the square below it. Then play and say the note names.

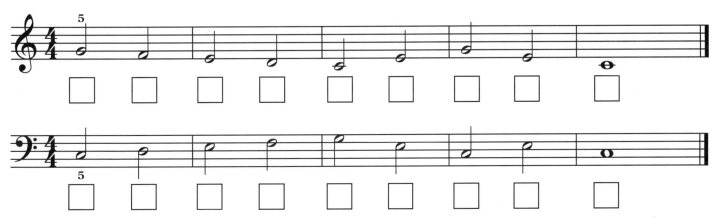

Staccato

Practice Directions
See page 75.

Staccato

A dot over or under a note tells you to play it *staccato*. This means the notes are played short, separated, and detached. Lift the finger off the key immediately after playing the note.

Staccato Warm-Up

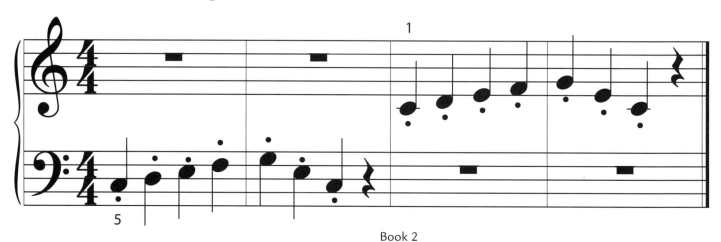

Bouncing on the Bus

Book 2
Track 7 (56)

C Position

Be sure to hold the whole notes 𝕠 for four full counts.

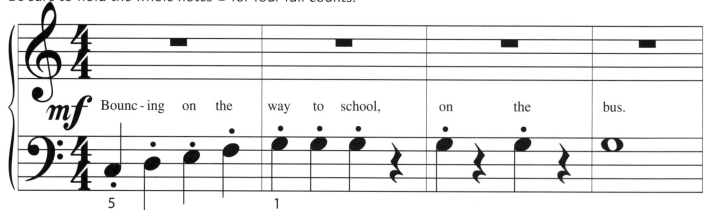

Bounc - ing   on   the   way   to   school,   on   the   bus.

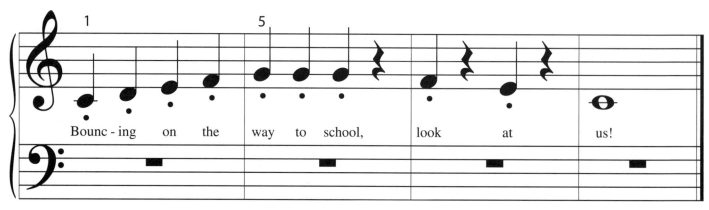

Bounc - ing   on   the   way   to   school,   look   at   us!

Practice Directions
See page 75.

Music Class

Book 2
Track 8 (57)

Middle C Position

Hold the whole notes for four full counts.

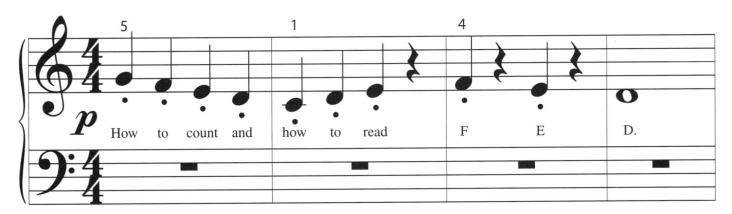

How to count and how to read F E D.

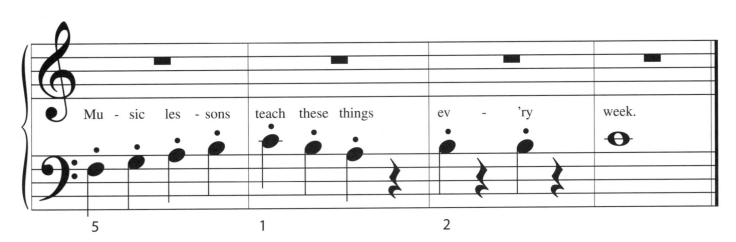

Mu - sic les - sons teach these things ev - 'ry week.

ACTIVITY: Review

Draw a line connecting the dots to match the symbol to its name.

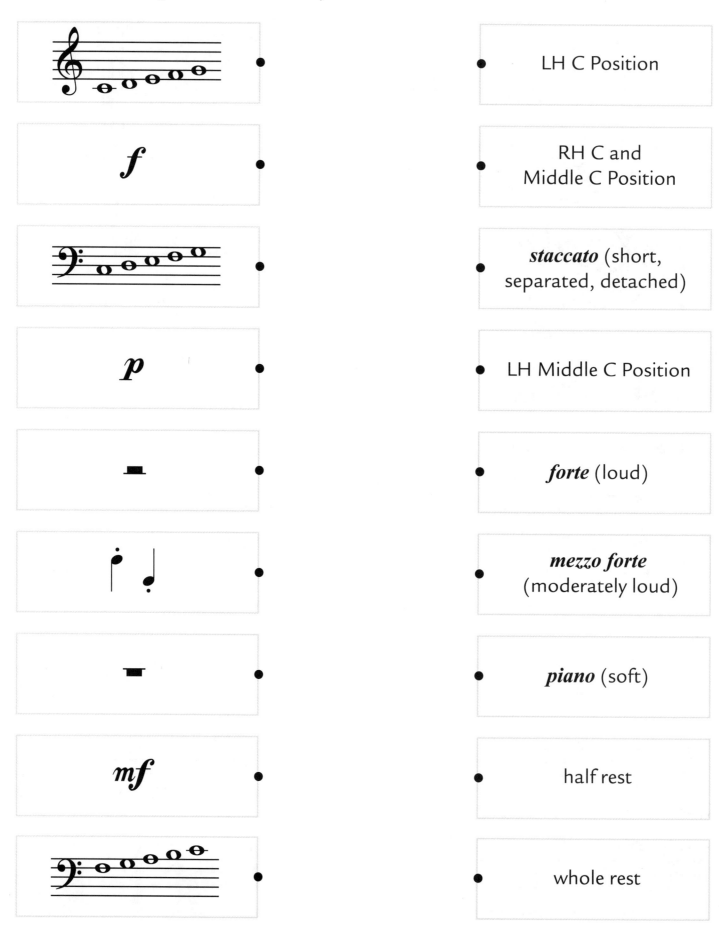

86

2nds

Practice Directions
See page 75.

A *2nd* is the same as a *step*. Do not skip any white keys or note names.

2nd

Intervals

The distance from one note to another note is called an *interval*. Intervals are numbered as 2nds, 3rds, 4ths, 5ths, and so on. A bigger number means the notes are further apart.

Steps and Seconds

Book 2
Track 9 (58)

C Position

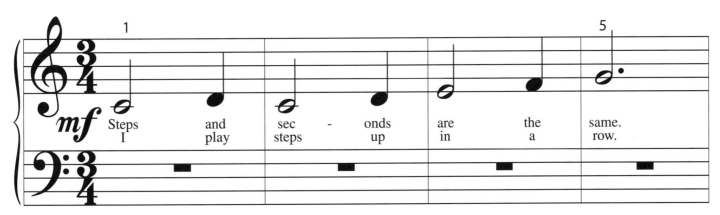

Steps   and   sec   -   onds   are   the   same.
I   play   steps   up   in   a   row.

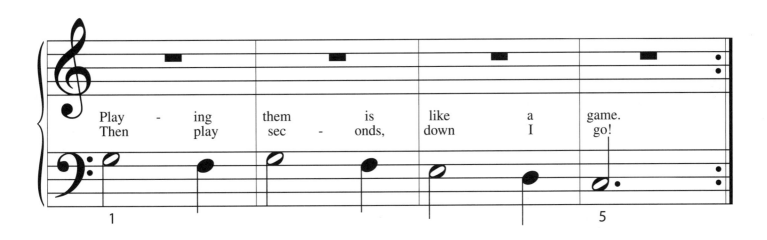

Play   -   ing   them   is   like   a   game.
Then   play   sec   -   onds,   down   I   go!

ACTIVITY: 2nds

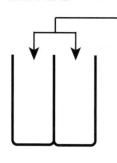

The distance from any white key to the next white key, up or down, is called a **2nd**.

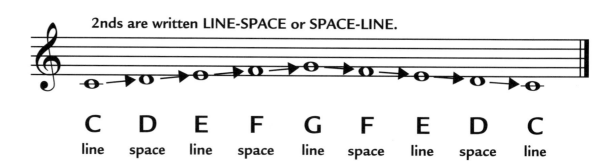

2nds are written LINE-SPACE or SPACE-LINE.

C	D	E	F	G	F	E	D	C
line	space	line	space	line	space	line	space	line

1. Draw a whole note UP a 2nd from the given note in each example below.
2. Write the name of each note in the square below it.

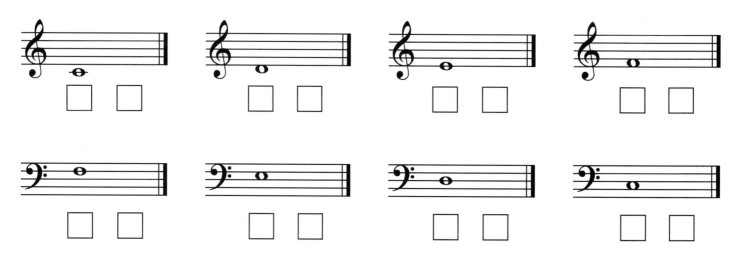

3. Draw a whole note DOWN a 2nd from the given note in each example below.
4. Write the name of each note in the square below it.

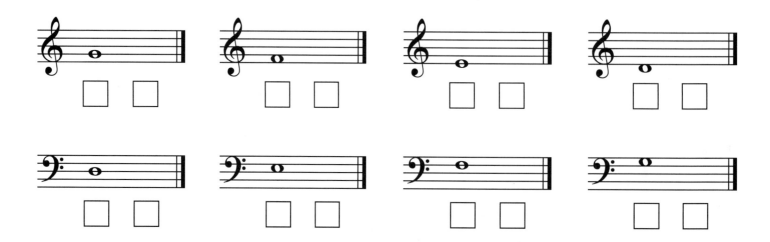

Practice Directions
See page 75.

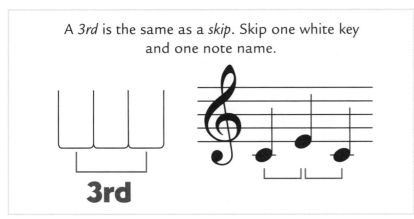

A *3rd* is the same as a *skip*. Skip one white key and one note name.

3rd

Thirds

Book 2
Track 10 (59)

C Position

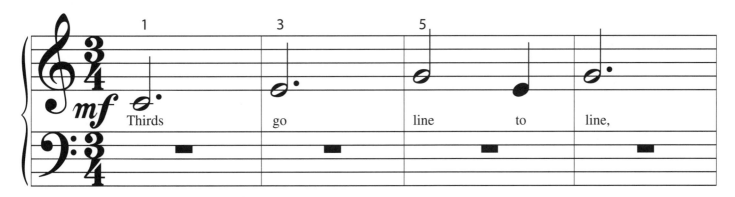

Thirds go line to line,

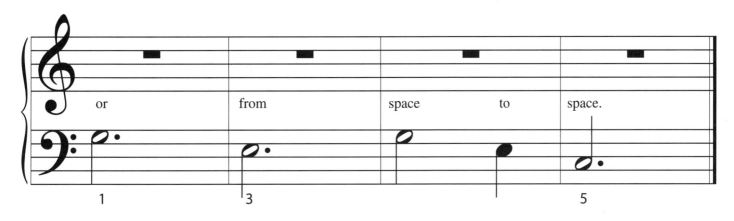

or from space to space.

ACTIVITY: 3rds

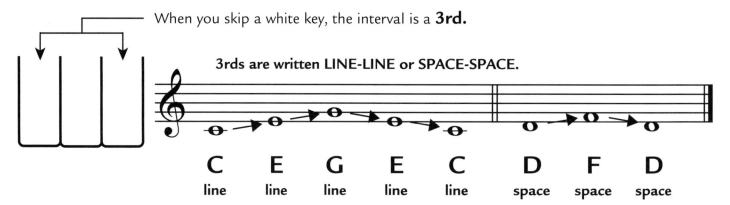

When you skip a white key, the interval is a **3rd.**

3rds are written LINE-LINE or SPACE-SPACE.

C	E	G	E	C	D	F	D
line	line	line	line	line	space	space	space

1. Draw a whole note UP a 3rd from the given note in each example below.
2. Write the name of each note in the square below it.

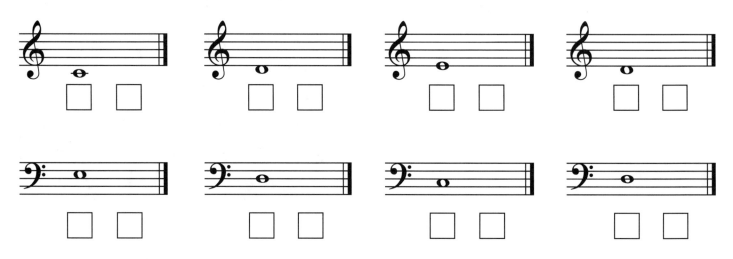

3. Draw a whole note DOWN a 3rd from the given note in each example below.
4. Write the name of each note in the square below it.

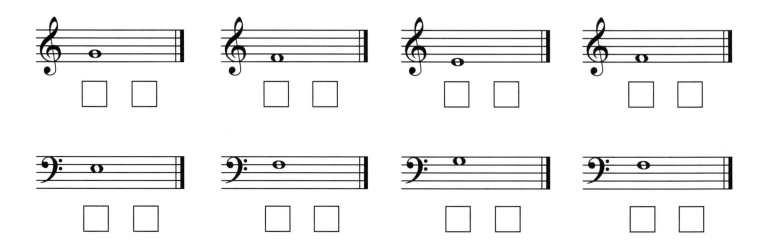

Legato

Practice Directions
See page 75.

To play *legato* means to play the notes smoothly connected. Hold every legato note right up until the next note is played, so there is no silence between them. A *slur* over or under notes means to play them legato.

Slur

Play legato.

Finger Steps

Book 2
Track 11 (60)

Middle C Position

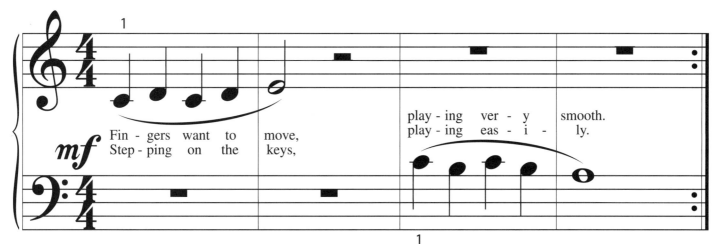

Fin - gers want to move,
Step - ping on the keys,
play - ing ver - y smooth.
play - ing eas - i - ly.

Finger Walk

Book 2
Track 12 (61)

C Position

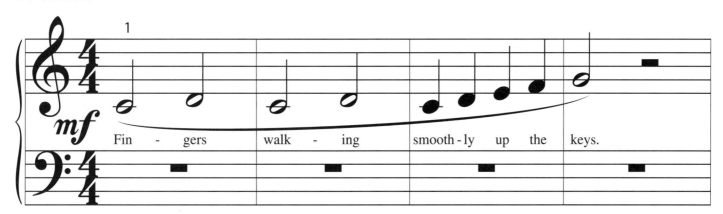

Fin - gers walk - ing smooth - ly up the keys.

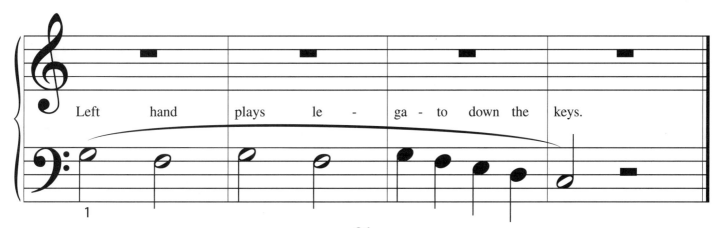

Left hand plays le - ga - to down the keys.

Practice Directions
See page 75.

Keyboard Dance

Book 2
Track 13 (62)

C Position

Most of the intervals in this piece are 3rds. Try to find some 2nds as well.
Remember to play *legato* and lift your hand for each quarter rest.

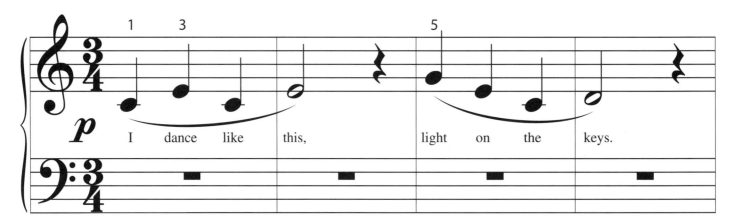

I   dance   like   this,   light   on   the   keys.

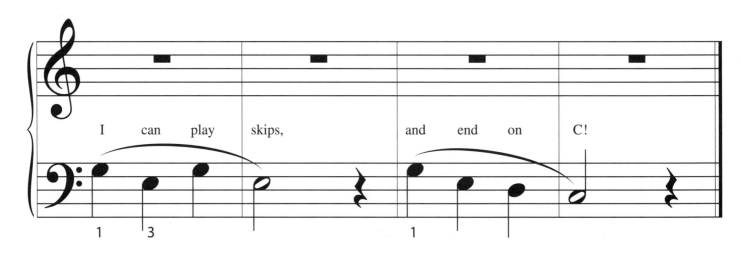

I   can   play   skips,   and   end   on   C!

Melodic and Harmonic Intervals

Melodic Interval

A *melody* is created when notes are played one at a time. The intervals between these notes are called *melodic intervals*.

Played separately.

Harmonic Interval

Notes that are played together make *harmony*. The intervals between notes played together are called *harmonic intervals*.

Played together.

A New Trick

RH C Position

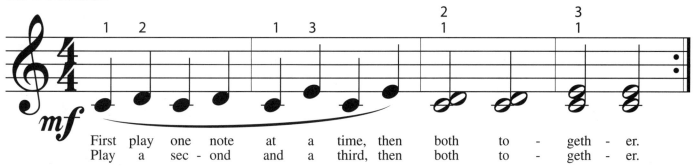

First play one note at a time, then both to - geth - er.
Play a sec - ond and a third, then both to - geth - er.

My Turn

LH C Position

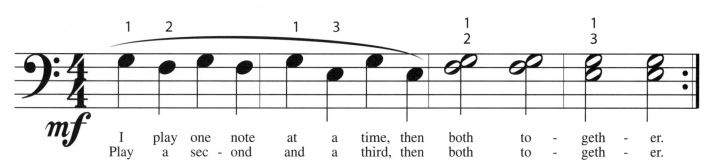

I play one note at a time, then both to - geth - er.
Play a sec - ond and a third, then both to - geth - er.

93

ACTIVITY: Melodic Intervals

Notes played SEPARATELY make a MELODY.
Intervals between these notes are MELODIC INTERVALS.

1. Write the names of the MELODIC INTERVALS (2nd or 3rd) in the boxes.

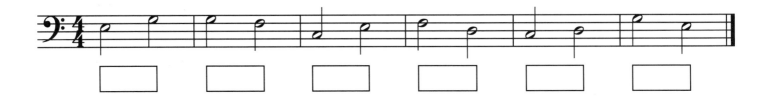

2. In the exercises below, identify the MELODIC INTERVALS in the C Position.
    • If the interval moves UP, write UP in the higher box above the staff.
    • If it moves DOWN, write DOWN in the higher box.
    • Write the name of the interval (2nd or 3rd) in the lower box.

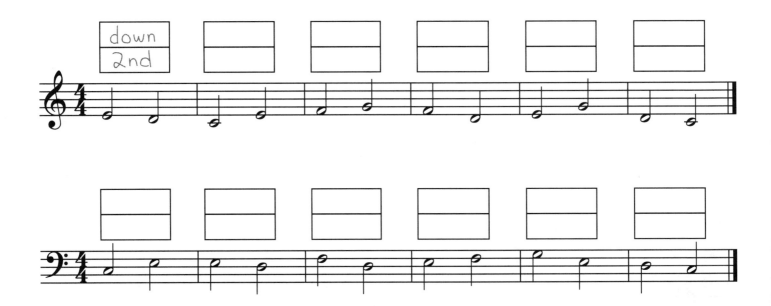

Practice Directions
See page 75.

Chopsticks

Book 2
Track 14 (63)

C Position

This little waltz is very popular with piano students. It was written around 1877.
Play harmonic 2nds and 3rds in the first line, and melodic 2nds and repeated
notes in the second line. Play the staccato notes with energy!

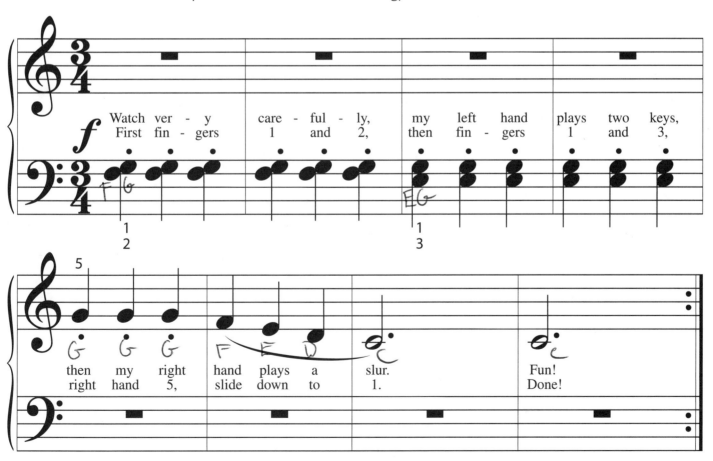

Watch ver - y care - ful - ly, my left hand plays two keys,
First fin - gers 1 and 2, then left fin - gers 1 two and 3,

then my right hand plays a slur. Fun!
right hand 5, slide down to 1. Done!

ACTIVITY: Harmonic Intervals

Notes played TOGETHER make HARMONY.
Intervals between these notes are HARMONIC INTERVALS.

1. Write the names of the HARMONIC INTERVALS (2nd or 3rd) in the boxes.

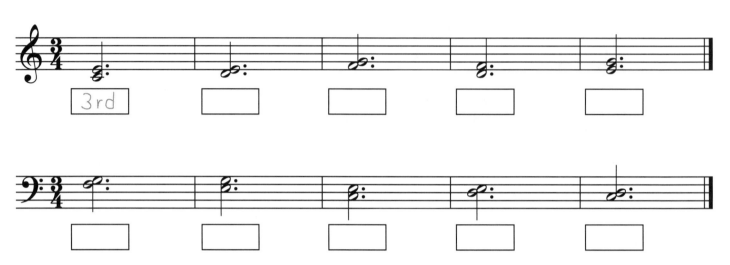

2. In the exercises below, write the names of the notes in the squares above the staff.
   Write the name of the lower note in the lower square; the name of the higher note
   in the higher square.

3. Write the names of the HARMONIC INTERVALS (2nd or 3rd) in the boxes below
   the staff.

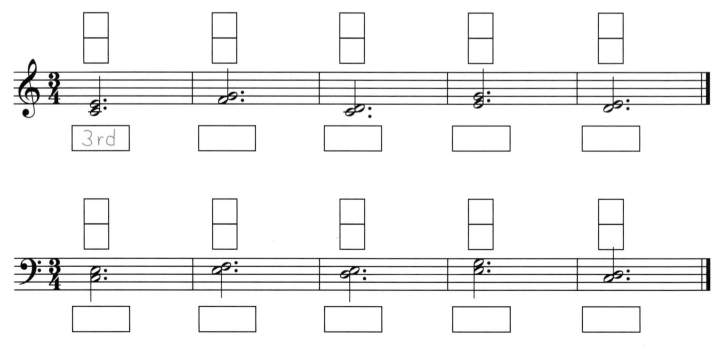

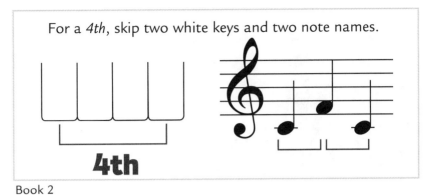

For a *4th*, skip two white keys and two note names.

4th

Fourths
Middle C Position

Book 2
Track 15 (64)

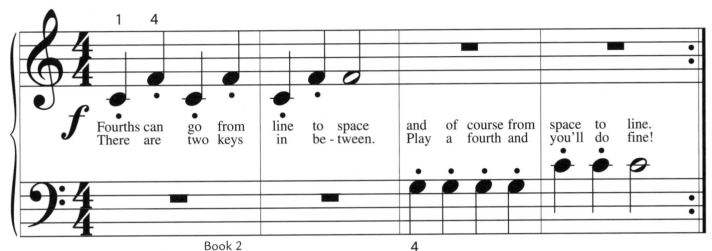

f

Fourths can go from line to space and of course from space to line.
There are two keys in be - tween. Play a fourth and you'll do fine!

Book 2
Track 16 (65)

My Fourth
C Position

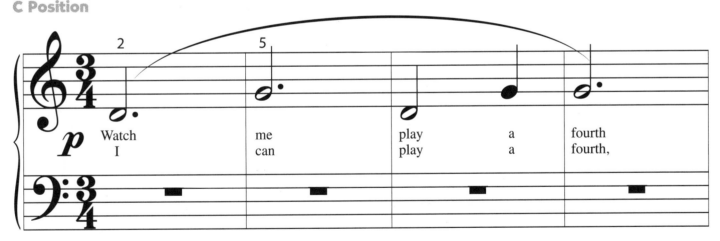

p

Watch me play a fourth
I can play a fourth,

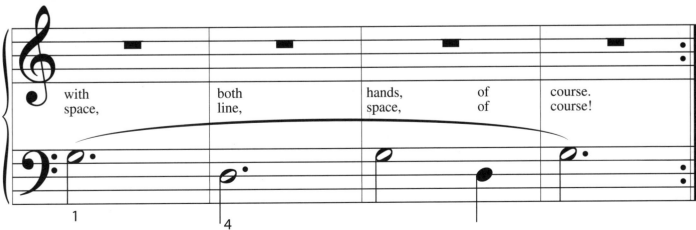

with both hands, of course.
space, line, space, of course!

Practice Directions
See page 75.

Big Ben

Book 2
Track 17 (66)

Middle C Position

Big Ben is the name of the giant clock in the bell tower of London's Westminster Palace.

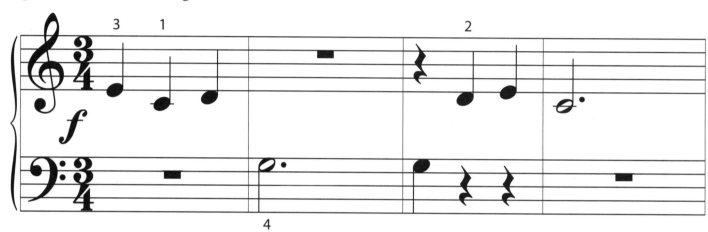

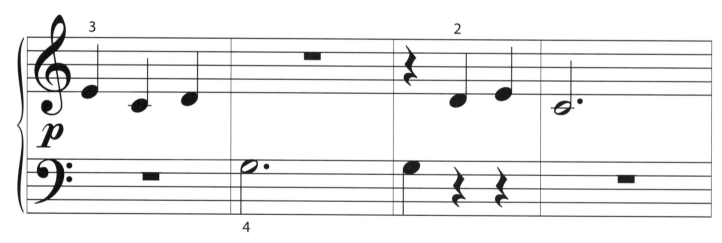

getting softer to the end

hold the right pedal down to the end

98

ACTIVITY: 4ths

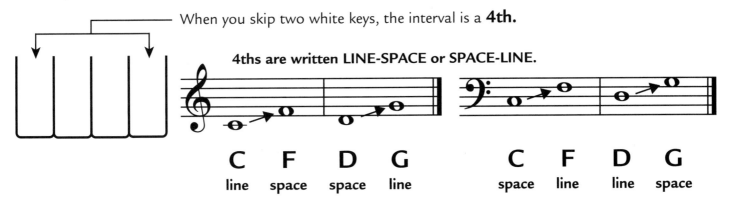

When you skip two white keys, the interval is a **4th.**

4ths are written LINE-SPACE or SPACE-LINE.

C	F	D	G
line	space	space	line

C	F	D	G
space	line	line	space

1. Draw a whole note UP a 4th from the given note in each example below.
2. Write the name of each note in the square below it.

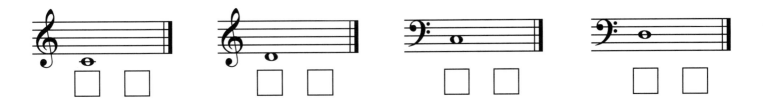

3. Draw a whole note DOWN a 4th from the given note in each example below.
4. Write the name of each note in the square below it.

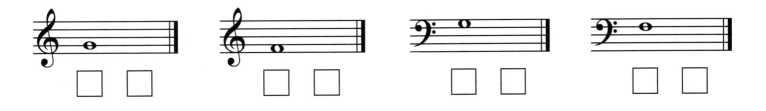

5. Circle each HARMONIC 4th.

Aura Lee

Book 2
Track 18 (67)

Middle C Position

Elvis Presley recorded this folk song as a
pop ballad called "Love Me Tender."

As the black-bird in the spring, 'neath the wil-low tree,

sat and piped I heard him sing, sing of Aur - a Lee.

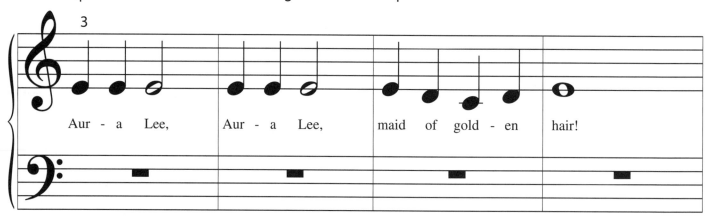

Aur - a Lee, Aur - a Lee, maid of gold - en hair!

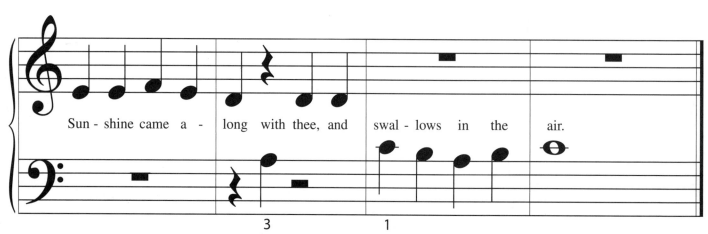

Sun-shine came a - long with thee, and swal - lows in the air.

Practice Directions
See page 75.

Song of the Volga Boatmen

Book 2
Track 19 (68)

Middle C Position

The first four-note group of this traditional Russian folk song is
frequently used in TV shows and movies.

Yo, ho, heave ho! Oh, yo, ho, heave ho! So

3rd

pull to - geth - er, yo, ho, heave ho!

4th

ACTIVITY:
Note and Interval Review

1. Write the name of each note in the square below it.

2. Using whole notes, draw the notes from the MIDDLE C POSITION in the TREBLE STAFF under the squares.

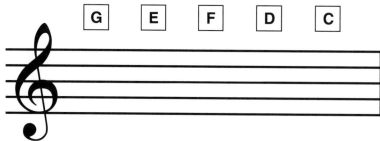

3. Using whole notes, draw the notes from the MIDDLE C POSITION in the BASS STAFF under the squares.

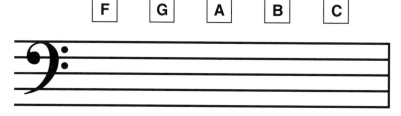

4. Draw a half note UP from the given note in each measure below to make the indicated melodic interval. Turn all the stems in the treble clef UP. Turn all the stems in the bass clef DOWN.

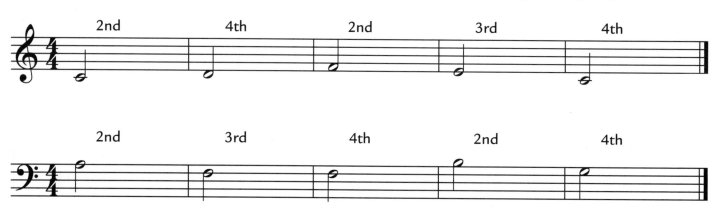

Here Comes the Bride

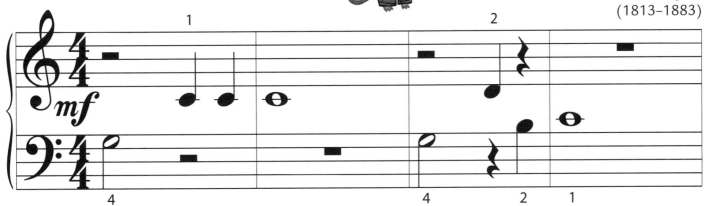

Middle C Position

This tune is the "Bridal Chorus" from the opera *Lohengrin*. It is often played during weddings as the bride walks down the aisle.

Book 2
Track 20 (69)

Practice Directions
See page 75.

Richard Wagner
(1813–1883)

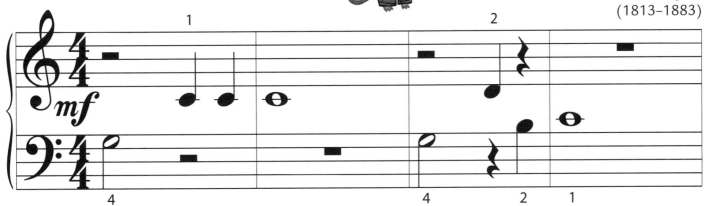

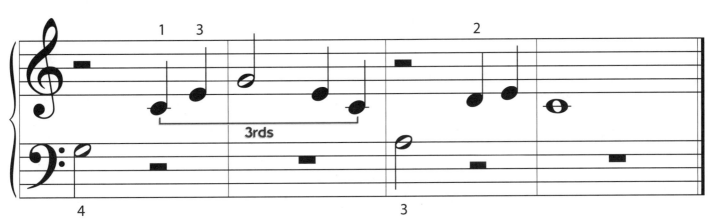

If You're Happy and You Know It

Book 2
 Track 21 (70)

Middle C Position

Practice Directions
See page 75.

* Optional: Tap on the wood of the piano with the right hand rather than clapping.

Fifths
Book 2
Track 22 (71)
C Position

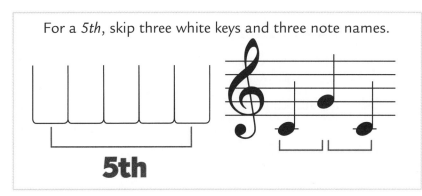

For a *5th*, skip three white keys and three note names.

5th

Skip three keys and play a fifth. 5 - 1, 1 - 5, play a fifth.
Space to space and line to line, I can play a fifth just fine.

The Bowing Song
Book 2
Track 23 (72)
C Position

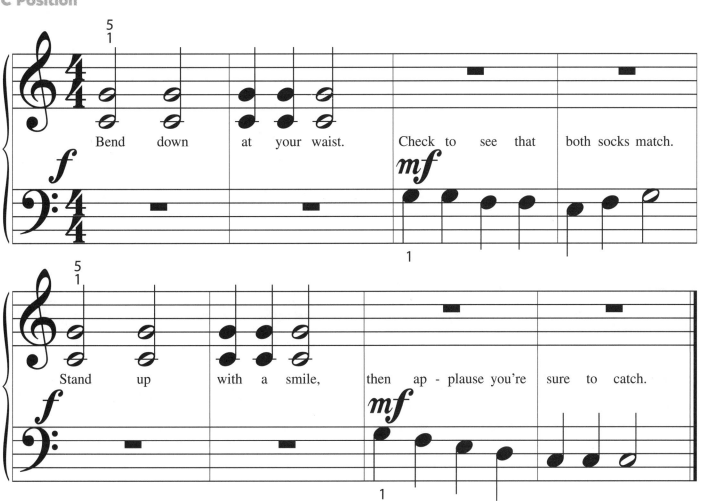

Bend down at your waist. Check to see that both socks match.

Stand up with a smile, then ap - plause you're sure to catch.

Love Somebody

Book 2
Track 24 (73)

C Position

This popular folk song was originally a fiddle tune used for square dancing. It is now thought of as a love ballad.

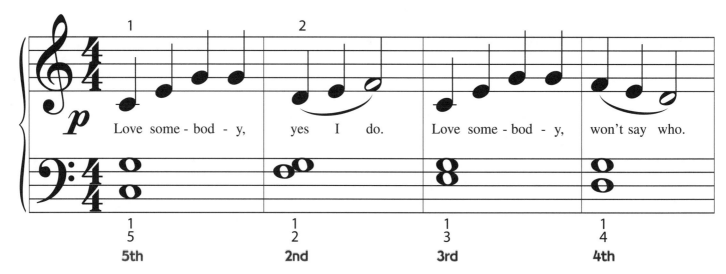

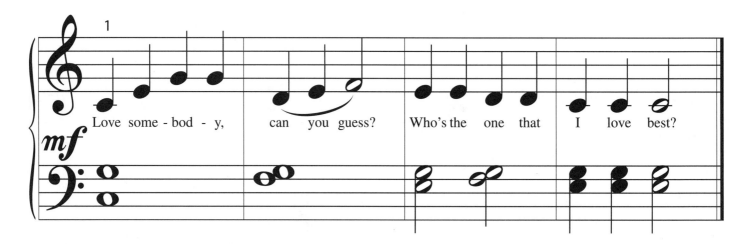

ACTIVITY: 5ths

When you skip three white keys, the interval is a **5th.**

5ths are written LINE-LINE or SPACE-SPACE.

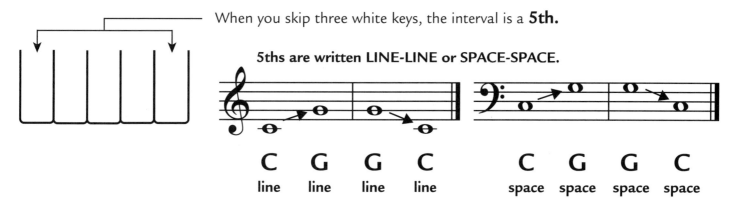

C	G	G	C		C	G	G	C
line	line	line	line		space	space	space	space

1. Draw a half note UP a 5th from each C and DOWN a 5th from each G on each staff below.
2. Write the name of each note in the square below it.

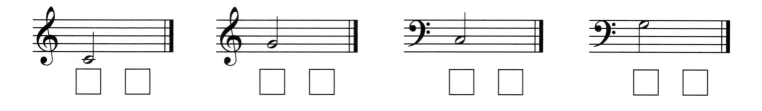

3. Draw a whole note ABOVE the given note in each measure below to make the indicated harmonic interval.
4. Write the names of the notes in the squares. Write the name of the lower note in the lower square; the name of the higher note in the higher square.

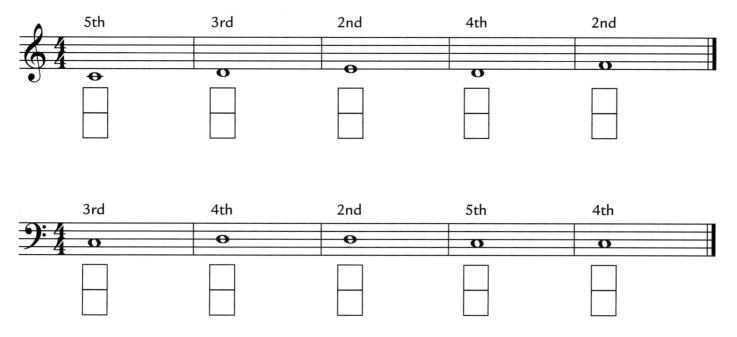

107

Practice Directions
See page 106.

Loud - Soft

f-p

When you see these dynamic signs together, it means to play *forte* the first time and *piano* when you repeat.

My Grand Finale

C Position

Book 2
Track 25 (74)

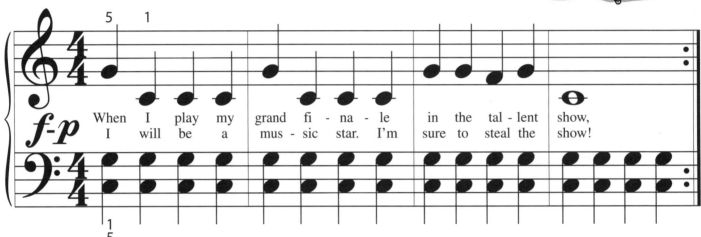

f-p

When I play my grand fi - na - le in the tal - lent show,
I will be a mus - sic star. I'm sure to steal the show!

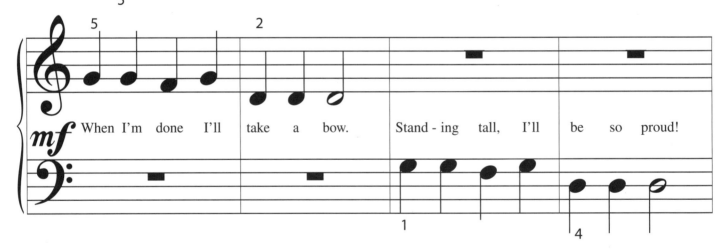

mf When I'm done I'll take a bow. Stand - ing tall, I'll be so proud!

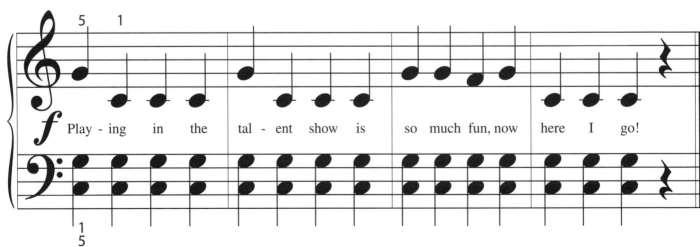

f Play - ing in the tal - ent show is so much fun, now here I go!

108

Practice Directions
See page 106.

Alouette

Book 2
Track 26 (75)

C Position

This famous French folk song is about a bird, the skylark. Be sure to name the harmonic intervals in the left hand.

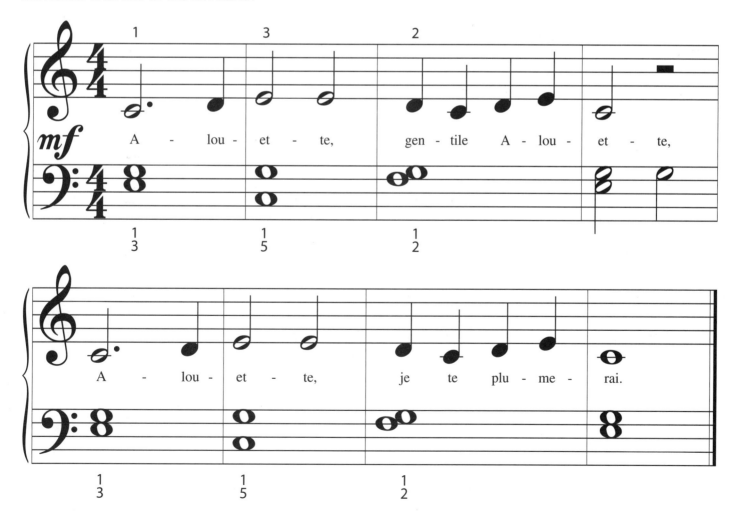

ACTIVITY:
Note and Interval Review

1. Write the name of each note in the square below it.

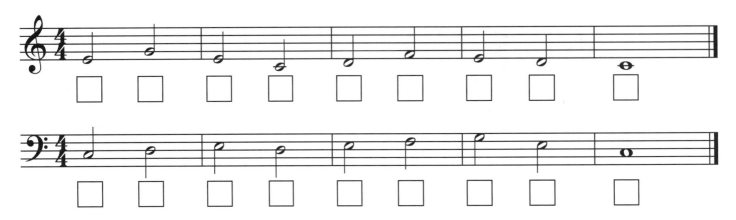

2. Using whole notes, draw the notes from the C POSITION in the TREBLE STAFF under the squares.

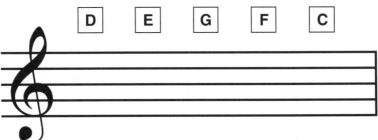

| D | E | G | F | C |

3. Using whole notes, draw the notes from the C POSITION in the BASS STAFF under the squares.

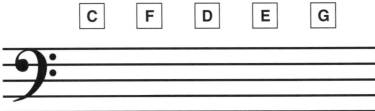

| C | F | D | E | G |

4. Draw a half note UP from the given note in each measure below to make the indicated melodic interval. Turn all the stems in the treble clef UP. Turn all the stems in the bass clef DOWN.

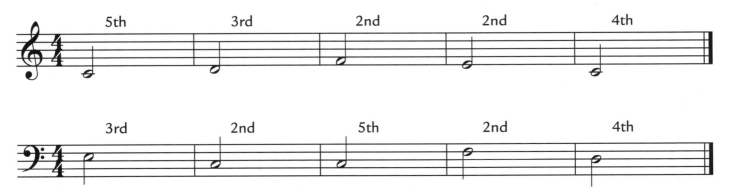

In the City

Book 2
Track 27 (76)

C Position

Practice Directions
See page 75.

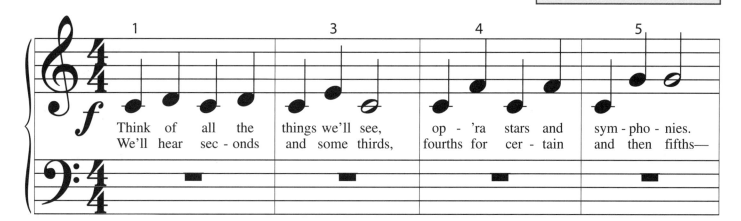

Think of all the things we'll see, op - 'ra stars and sym - pho - nies.
We'll hear sec - onds and some thirds, fourths for cer - tain and then fifths—

Art mu - se - ums, bal - let, too, there's so much to see and do.
all the in - ter - vals we know on the field trip as we go.

Time to Go!

Book 2
Track 28 (77)

C Position

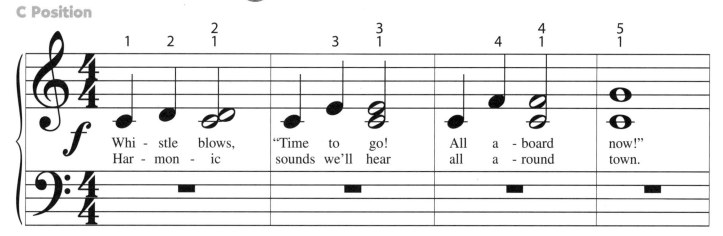

Whi - stle blows, "Time to go! All a - board now!"
Har - mon - ic sounds we'll hear all a - round town.

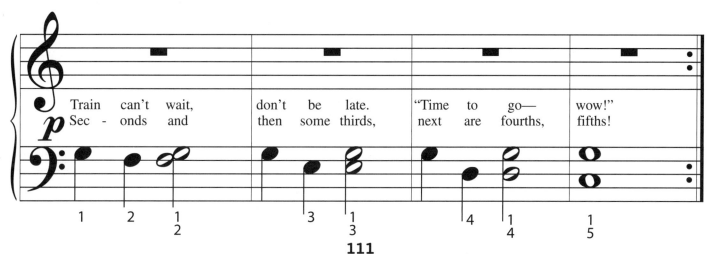

Train can't wait, don't be late. "Time to go— wow!"
Sec - onds and then some thirds, next are fourths, fifths!

111

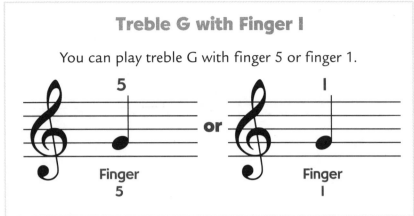

Treble G with Finger 1

You can play treble G with finger 5 or finger 1.

Finger 5 **or** Finger 1

The Amazing Pianist

Book 2
Track 29 (78)

Practice Directions
See page 75.

Middle C Position

In this piece, treble G is sometimes played with finger 5, and sometimes with finger 1. Shift your hand smoothly across the keys on the rests.

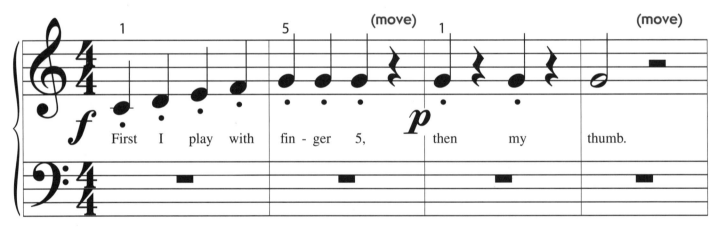

First I play with fin - ger 5, then my thumb.

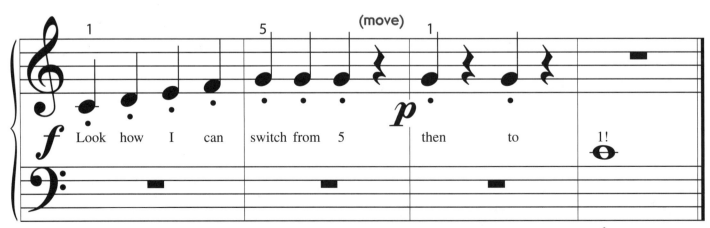

Look how I can switch from 5 then to 1!

Treble Clef A

Practice Directions
See page 75.

My Advice

Circle each treble clef A
before you play.

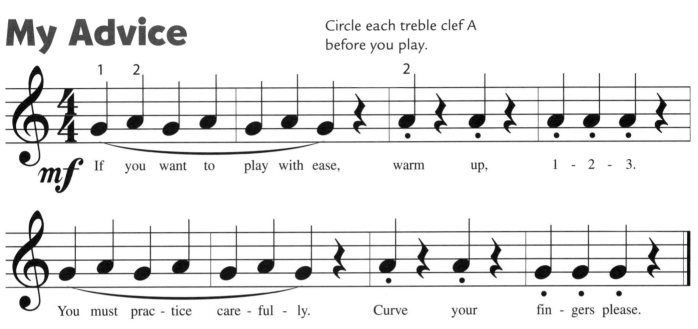

mf If you want to play with ease, warm up, 1 - 2 - 3.

You must prac - tice care - ful - ly. Curve your fin - gers please.

Treble Clef B

My Warm-Up

Book 2
Track 30 (79)

Circle each treble clef B
before you play.

f Warm - ing up on the keys, eas - i - ly.

I can play grace - ful - ly. Look at me!

ACTIVITY: G-A-B in Treble Clef

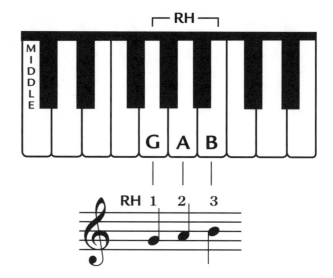

1. Using quarter notes, draw G five more times.

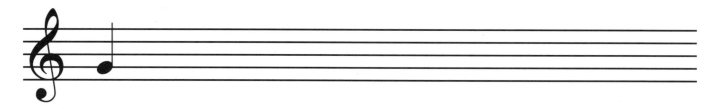

2. Using half notes, draw A five more times.

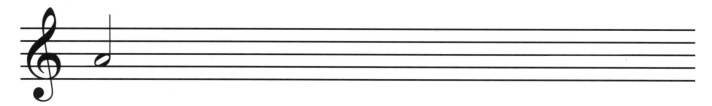

3. Using whole notes, draw B five more times.

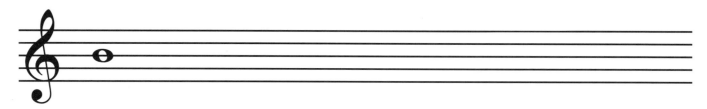

4. Draw lines connecting the dots
   on the matching boxes.

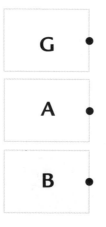

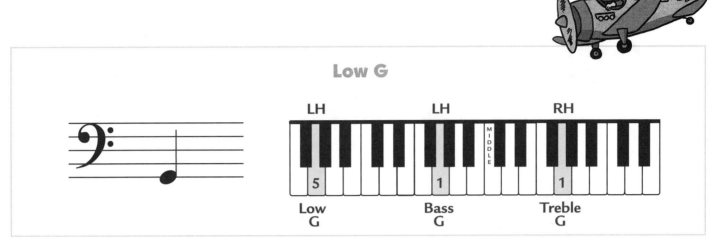

Low G

Three Gs

Book 2
Track 31 (80)

Remember to shift your hand smoothly across the keys during the rest to get to the new position.

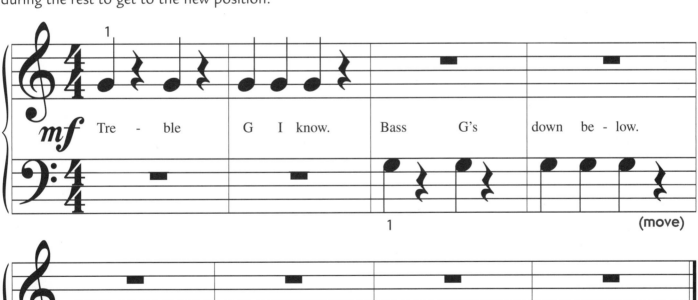

mf Tre - ble   G I know.   Bass   G's   down be - low.

(move)

Low   G   is brand - new.   I know three Gs   now, do you?

115

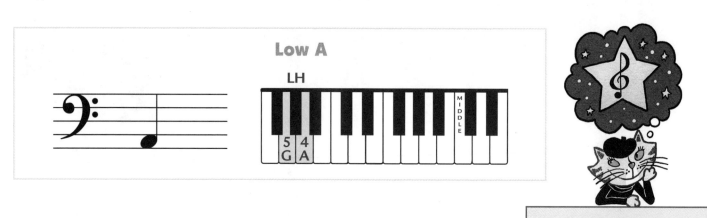

Low A

Music Star

Circle each low A before you play.

Practice Directions
See page 75.

Some-day I will be a star   so   I'll   prac - tice hard.

Play in plac - es near and far   I'm   a   mu - sic star!

Low B

Page by Page

Book 2
Track 32 (81)

Circle each low B before you play.

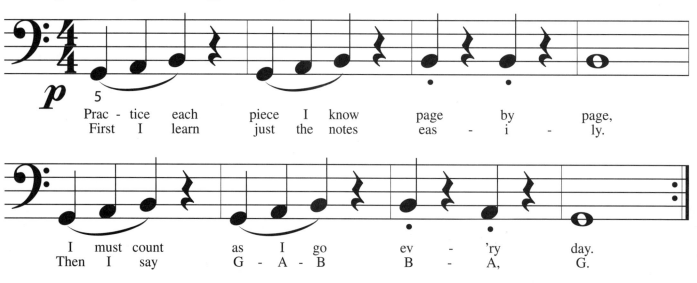

Prac - tice each   piece I know   page   by   page,
First I learn   just the notes   eas - i - ly.

I must count   as I go   ev - 'ry   day.
Then I say   G - A - B   B - A,   G.

116

ACTIVITY: G-A-B in Bass Clef

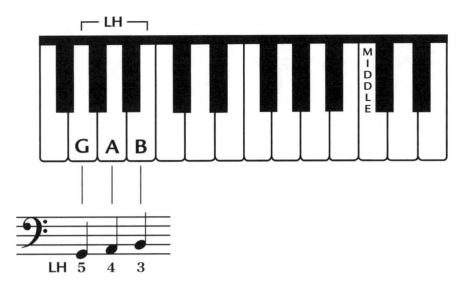

1. Using whole notes, draw G five more times.

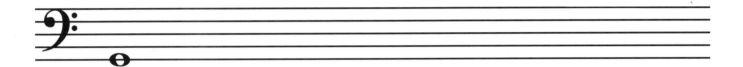

2. Using half notes, draw A five more times.

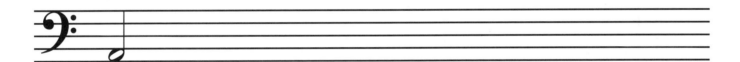

3. Using quarter notes, draw B five more times.

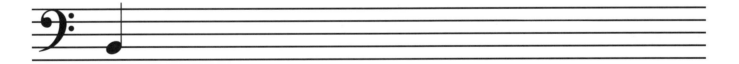

4. Draw lines connecting the dots on the matching boxes.

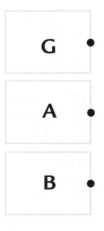
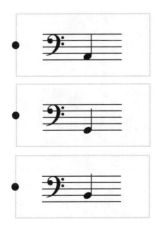

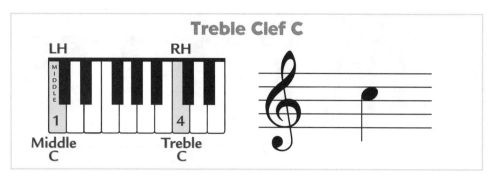

Treble Clef C

Yes, I Can!

Yes, yes, yes I can, play two Cs and sound so grand!

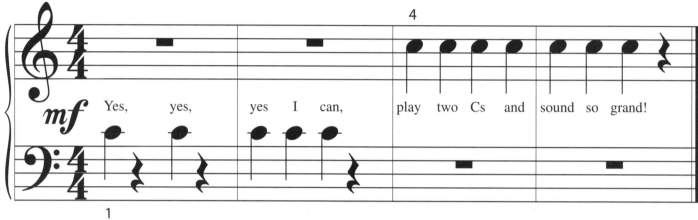

Treble Clef D

Book 2
Track 33 (82)

Treble D

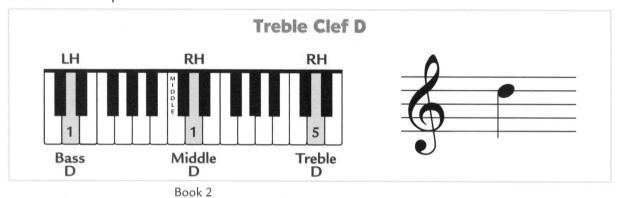

First I play down low. Mid - dle D I know.

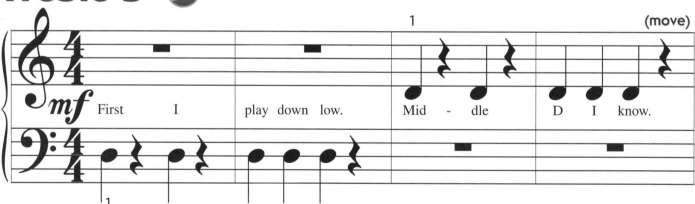

Treb - le D is new, I will play it just for you.

G Position for RH

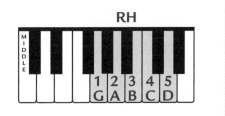

This hand position uses the notes you just learned starting with your thumb on G above middle C.

Waiting for the School Bus

Book 2
Track 34 (83)

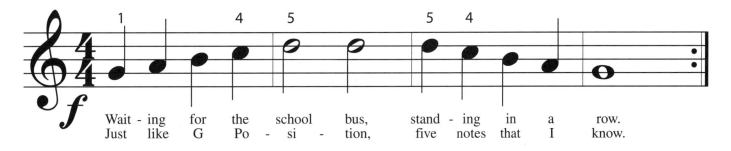

Wait - ing for the school bus, stand - ing in a row.
Just like G Po - si - tion, five notes that I know.

Traffic Lights

Book 2
Track 35 (84)

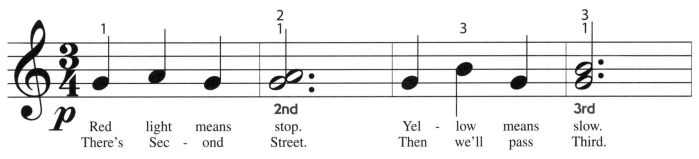

Red light means stop. Yel - low means slow.
There's Sec - ond Street. Then we'll pass Third.

2nd **3rd**

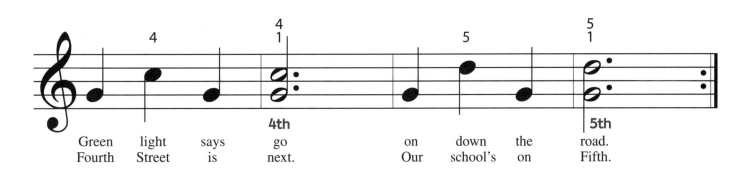

Green light says go on down the road.
Fourth Street is next. Our school's on Fifth.

4th **5th**

ACTIVITY:
G Position for RH

1. Print the letter names for the RH G POSITION on the keyboard.

2. Draw a line to connect each note on the staff to the appropriate key on the keyboard.

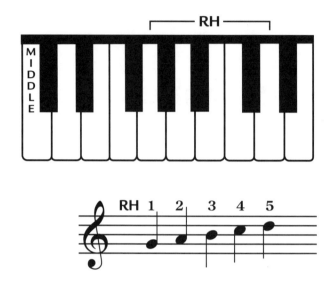

3. Draw lines connecting the dots on the matching boxes.

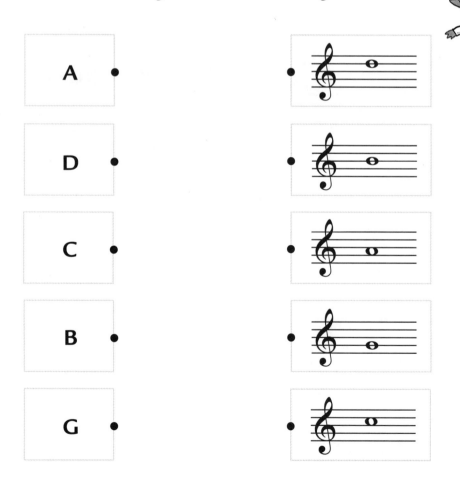

G Position for LH

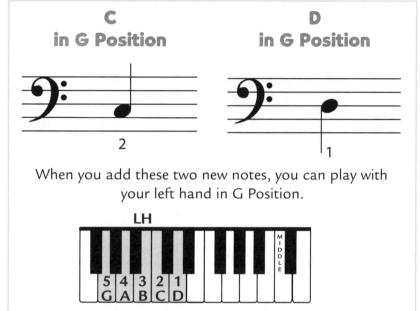

C in G Position

D in G Position

When you add these two new notes, you can play with your left hand in G Position.

LH

5 4 3 2 1
G A B C D

At the Art Museum

Book 2
Track 36 (85)

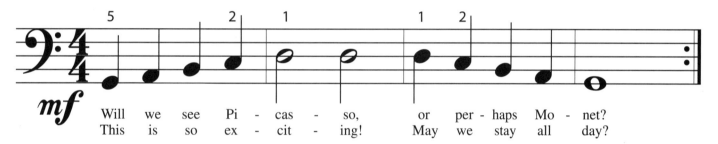

mf

Will we see Pi - cas - so, or per - haps Mo - net?
This is so ex - cit - ing! May we stay all day?

Stop, Look and Listen

Book 2
Track 37 (86)

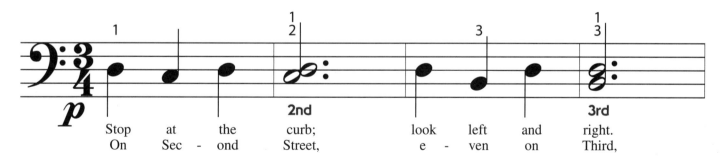

p

2nd
Stop at the curb; look left and right.
On Sec - ond Street, e - ven on Third,

3rd

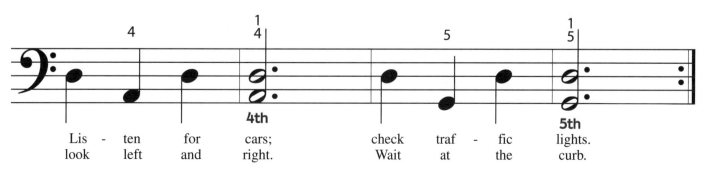

4th
Lis - ten for cars; check traf - fic lights.
look left and right. Wait at the curb.

5th

ACTIVITY:
G Position for LH

1. Print the letter names for the LH G POSITION on the keyboard.

2. Draw a line to connect each note on the staff to the appropriate key on the keyboard.

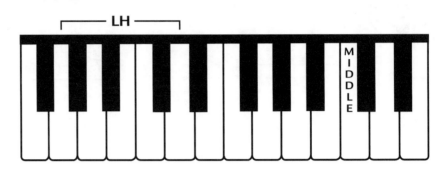

LH 5   4   3   2   1

3. Draw lines connecting the dots on the matching boxes.

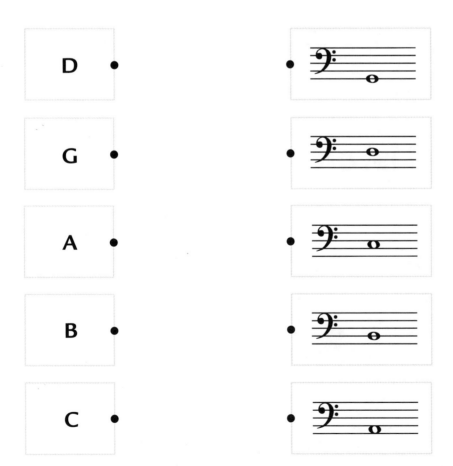

D •

G •

A •

B •

C •

G Position for Both Hands

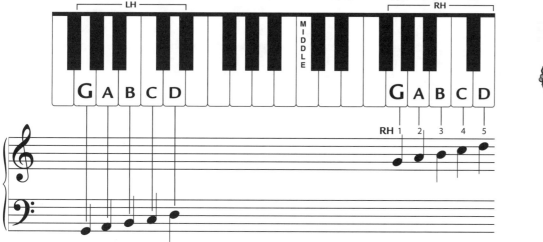

Tempo

The *tempo* is the speed of a piece of music. A tempo marking is often placed above the time signature to tell you to play fast or slow. Like dynamics, tempo marks are often Italian words.

Moderate Tempo

Moderato

(mah-deh-RAH-tow)

Play at a moderate speed, not too fast and not to slow.

Practice Directions
See page 106.

Ode to Joy
(Theme from the Ninth Symphony)
G Position

Book 2
 Track 38 (87)

Ludwig van Beethoven
(1770–1827)

ACTIVITY:
G Position on the Grand Staff

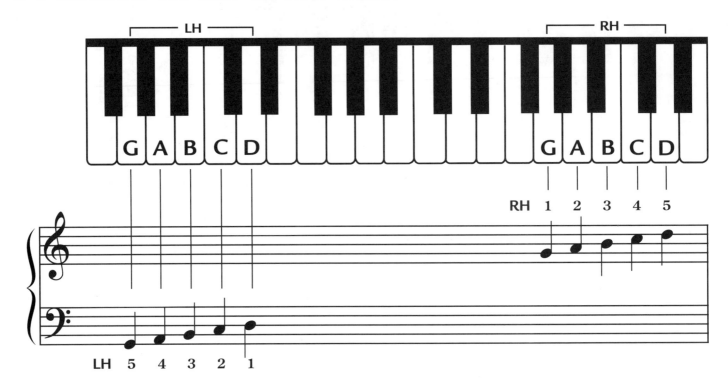

1. Using whole notes, draw the LH notes from G Position in the BASS staff under the squares.

2. Using whole notes, draw the RH notes from G Position in the TREBLE staff over the squares.

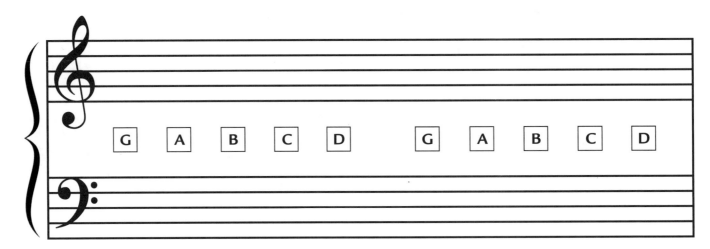

3. Write the name of each note in the square below it. Then play and say the note names.

Flat Sign

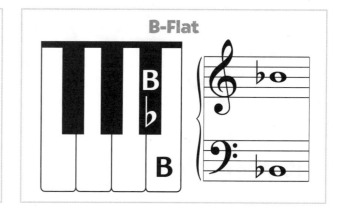

Flat Sign

When a flat sign appears next to a note, it means to play the next key to the left, whether black or white. The flat sign applies to that note for the rest of the measure.

B-Flat

Flat Warm-Up

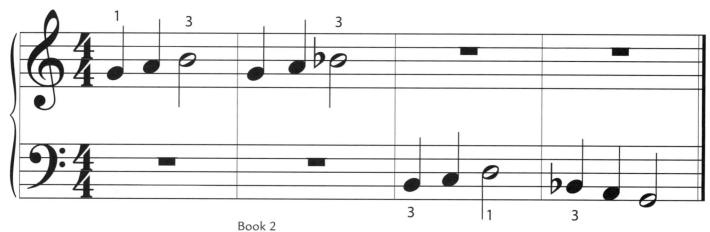

Tire Trouble

Book 2
Track 39 (88)

G Position (with B♭)

Moderato

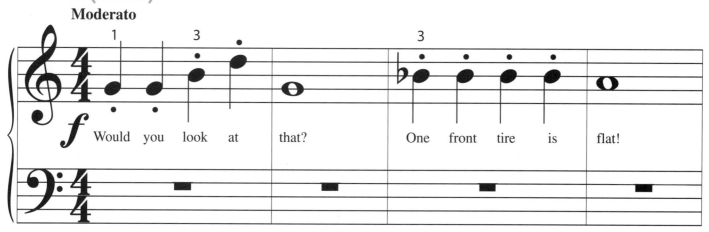

Would you look at that? One front tire is flat!

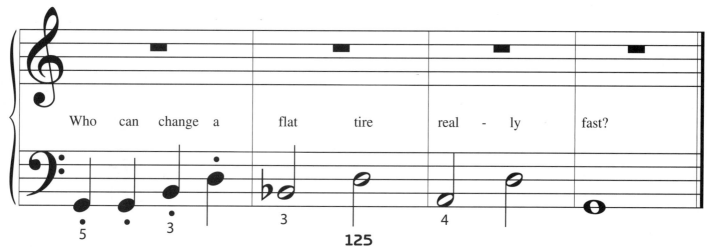

Who can change a flat tire real - ly fast?

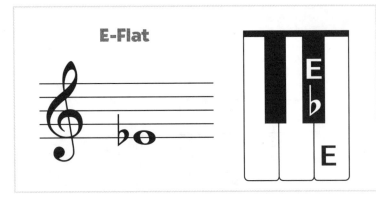

E-Flat

Fast Tempo

Allegro

(ah-LEG-row)

Play fast.

Flat Warm-Up

In a Flash

Book 2
Track 40 (89)

Middle C Position (with B♭ and E♭)

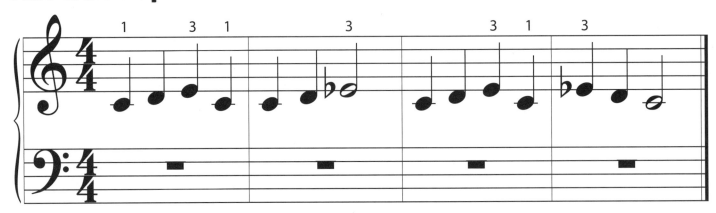

Allegro

See the driv - er fix this flat. He can fix it fast.
He has prac - ticed real - ly hard. He has prac - ticed well.

He is fin - ished in a flash. No more flats!
He is good at what he does. I can tell.

Oh, Dear! What Can the Matter Be?

Practice Directions
See page 75.

Middle C Position (with B♭)

127

ACTIVITY: Flat

1. Draw a FLAT (♭) before each B on the staffs below.

2. Write the name of each note in the square below it.

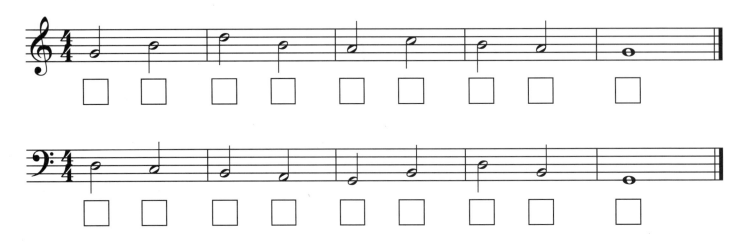

3. Draw lines connecting the dots, to match the name of the flatted note to its location on the keytboard.

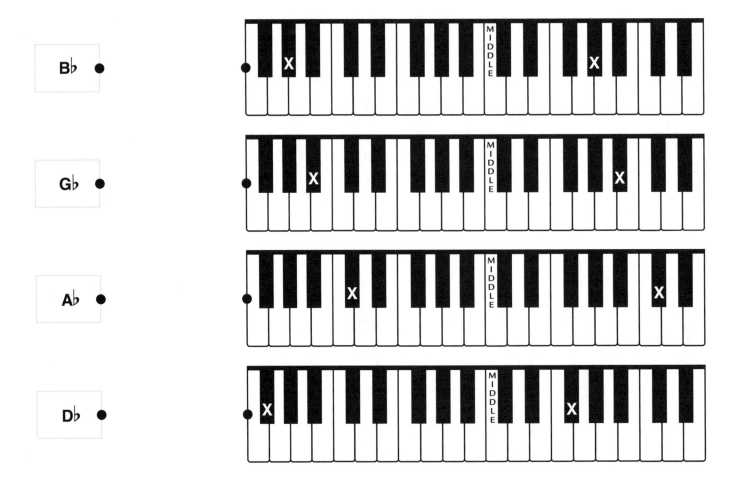

Sharp Sign

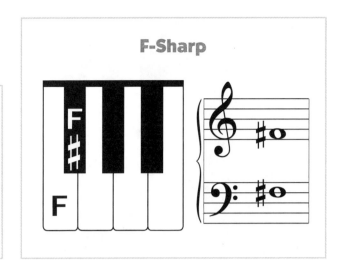

F-Sharp

Sharp Sign

♯

When a sharp sign appears next to a note, it means to play the next key to the right, whether black or white. The sharp sign applies to that note for the rest of the measure.

Sharp Warm-Up

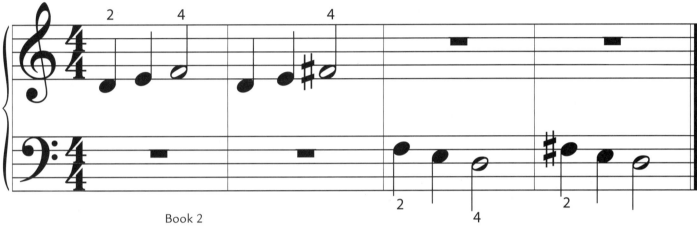

The Test

Book 2
Track 42 (91)

C Position (with F♯)

Moderately slow

We have a test. We must re - view.
We must be sharp to take our test.

You quiz me. I'll quiz you.
so we can do our best.

129

Practice Directions
See page 75.

D-Sharp

Favorite Composers

Book 2
Track 43 (92)

Middle C Position (with D♯)

Allegro

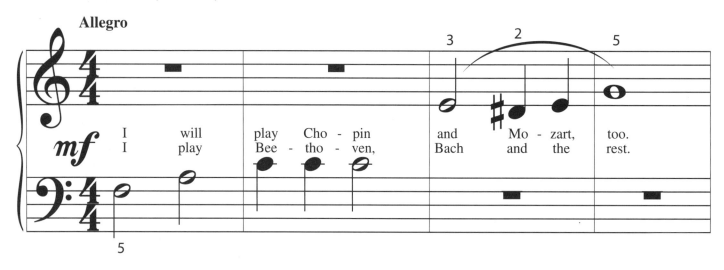

mf

I will play Cho - pin
I will play Bee - tho - ven,

and Mo - zart, too.
Bach and the rest.

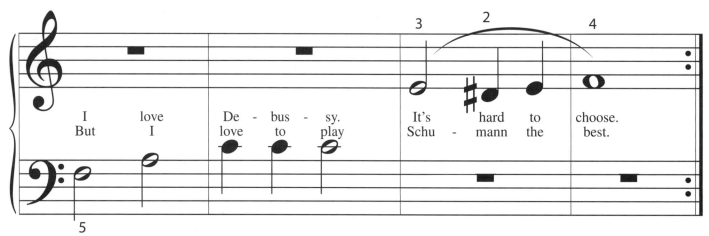

I love De - bus - sy.
But I love to play

It's hard to choose.
Schu - mann the best.

130

Can Can

Book 2
Track 44 (93)

(from Orpheus in the Underworld)

Middle C Position (with F♯)

Jacques Offenbach
(1819–1880)

Allegro

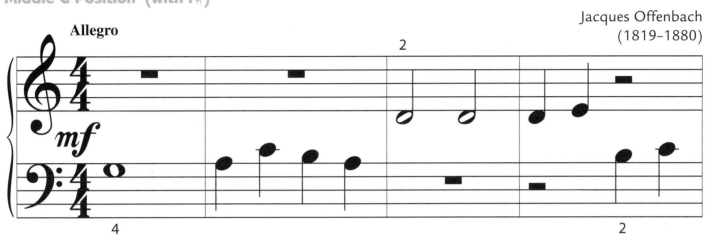

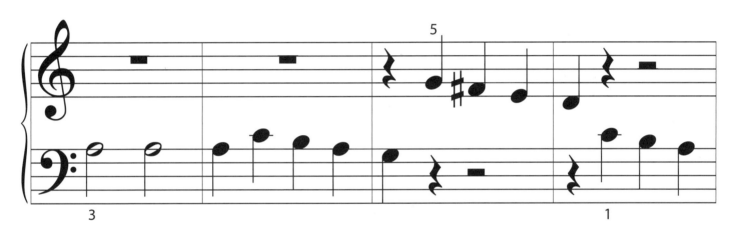

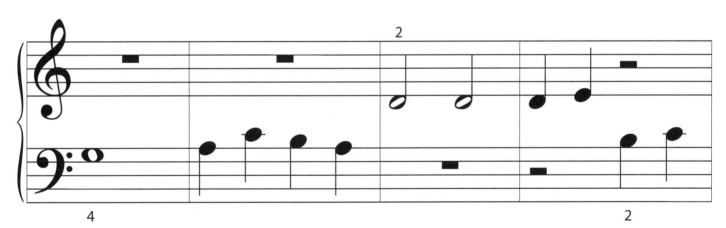

ACTIVITY: Sharp

1. Draw a SHARP (♯) before each C on the staffs below.

2. Write the name of each note in the square below it.

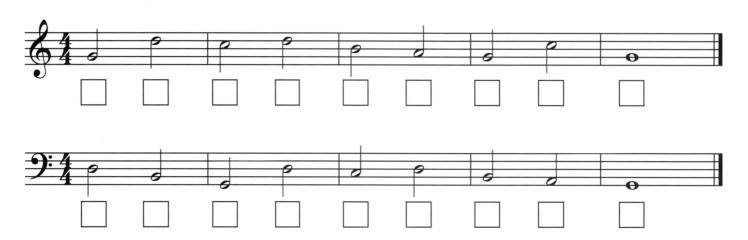

3. Draw lines connecting the dots, to match the name of the flatted note to its location on the keyboard.

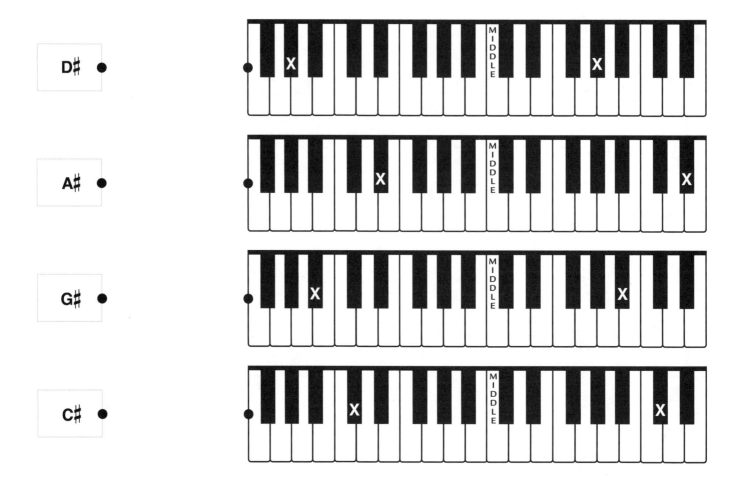

Tied Notes

A *tie* is a curved line that connects two notes on the same space or line. Play once, and hold for the combined value of both notes.

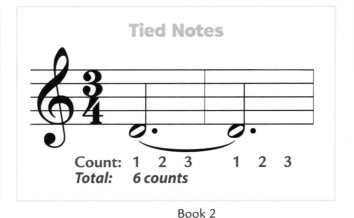

Tied Notes

Count: 1 2 3   1 2 3
Total: **6 counts**

Practice Directions
See page 75.

The Piano Concert
Book 2
Track 45 (94)

C Position

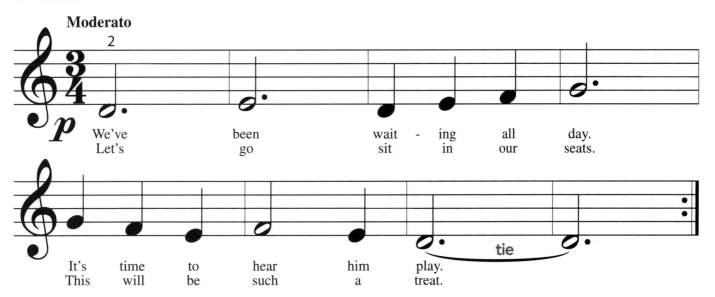

We've ... been ... wait - ing ... all ... day.
Let's ... go ... sit ... in ... our ... seats.

It's time to hear him play. tie
This will be such a treat.

Flying Fingers
Book 2
Track 46 (95)

Middle C Position (with B♭)

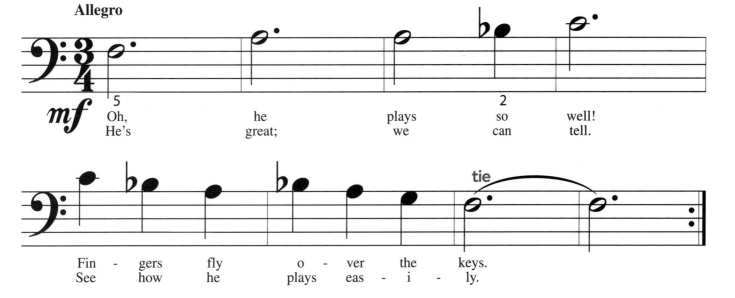

Oh, ... he ... plays ... so ... well!
He's ... great; ... we ... can ... tell.

Fin - gers fly o - ver the keys. tie
See how he plays eas - i - ly.

Theme from Swan Lake

Book 2
Track 47 (96)

Middle C Position

Peter Ilyich Tchaikovsky
(1840–1893)

Moderately slow

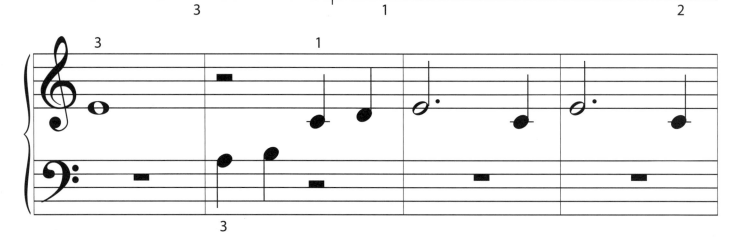

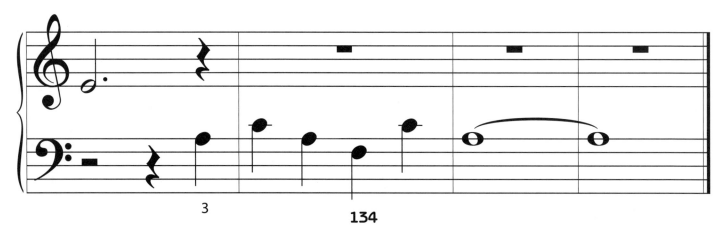

ACTIVITY:
Note and Interval Review in Treble Clef

1. Draw lines connecting the dots to the matching boxes.

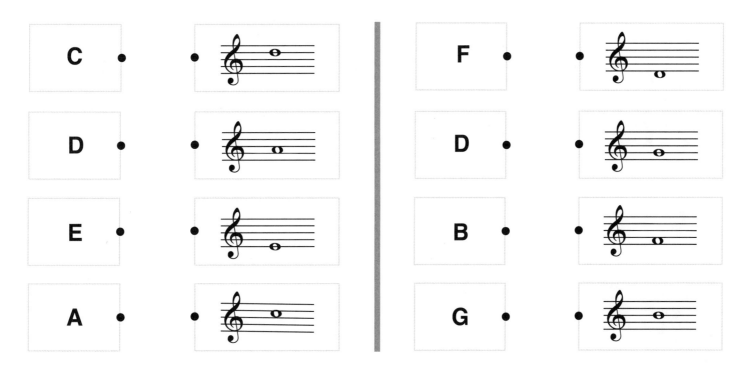

2. Draw a half note BELOW the given note to make the indicated melodic interval.
   Turn all the stems UP.

3. Write the name of each note in the square below it.

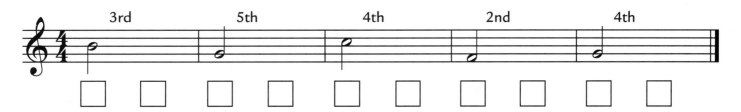

4. Draw a whole note ABOVE the given note to make the indicated harmonic interval.

5. Write the names of the notes in the squares. Write the name of the lower note in
   the lower square; the name of the higher note in the higher square.

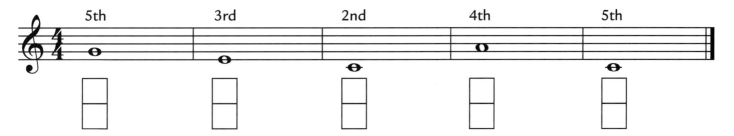

Dance of the Reed Flutes

Middle C Position

Peter Ilyich Tchaikovsky
(1840–1893)

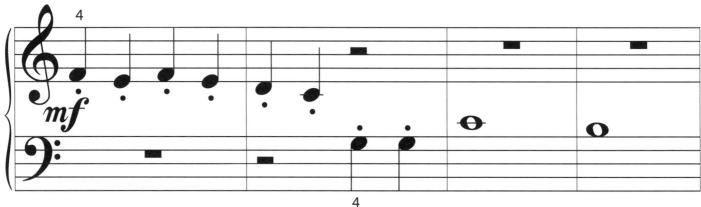

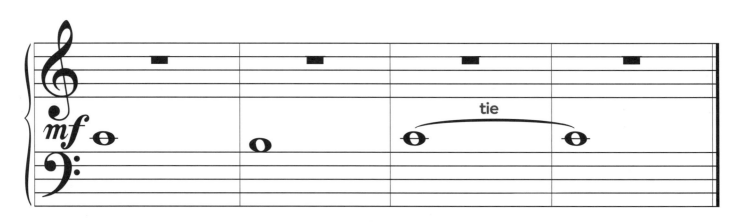

When the Saints Go Marching In

C Position

Moderato

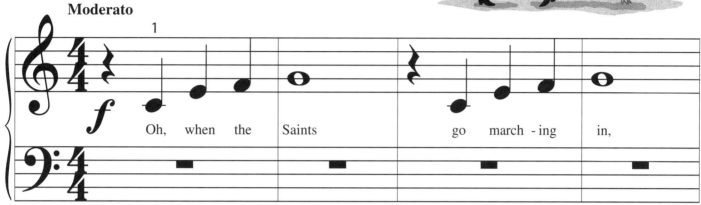

Oh, when the Saints   go march - ing   in,

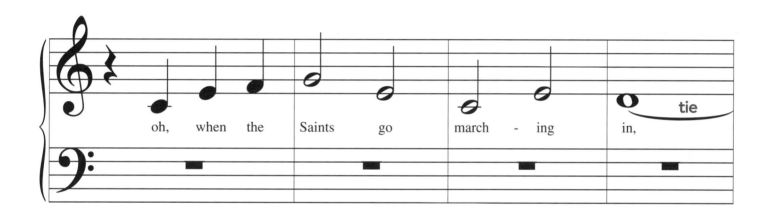

oh, when the Saints go march - ing in,   *tie*

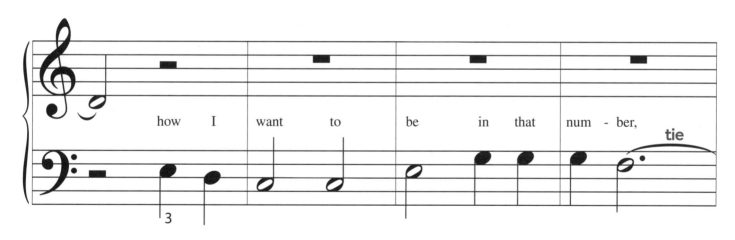

how I want to be in that num - ber,   *tie*

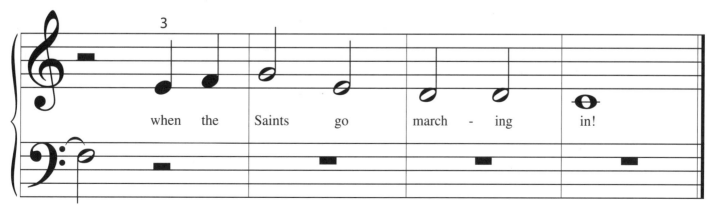

when the Saints go march - ing in!

ACTIVITY:
Note and Interval Review in Bass Clef

1. Draw lines connecting the dots to the matching boxes.

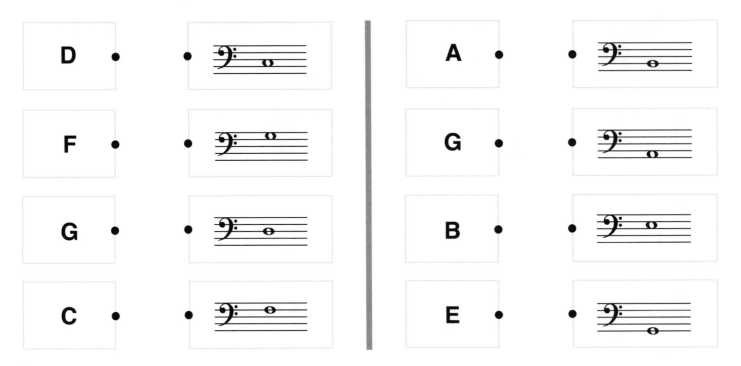

2. Draw a half note BELOW the given note to make the indicated melodic interval.
   Turn all the stems UP.

3. Write the name of each note in the square below it.

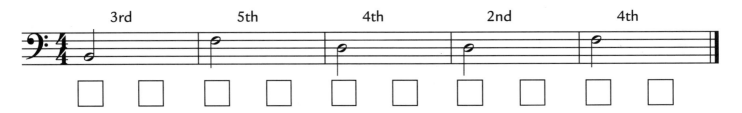

4. Draw a whole note ABOVE the given note to make the indicated harmonic interval.

5. Write the names of the notes in the squares. Write the name of the lower note in
   the lower square; the name of the higher note in the higher square.

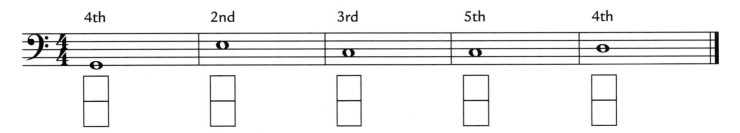

Music Matching Games

Symbols

Draw a line to match each symbol on the left to its name on the right.

1.

2.

3.

4.

5.

6.

7. Moderato

8. ♭

9. ♯

10. Allegro

11.

slur (play legato)

3rd

sharp

staccato

2nd

4th

flat

moderate tempo

tied notes

5th

fast tempo

Treble Clef Notes

Draw a line to match each treble clef note on the left to its correct letter name on the right.

1.

2.

3.

4.

5.

G

A

B

C

D

Bass Clef Notes

Draw a line to match each bass clef note on the left to its correct letter name on the right.

1.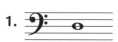

2.

3.

4.

5.

G

A

B

C

D

Answer Key

Treble Clef Notes

1. B
2. A
3. D
4. G
5. C

Bass Clef Notes

1. D
2. G
3. B
4. C
5. A

Symbols

1. staccato
2. 2nd
3. 3rd
4. slur
5. 4th
6. 5th
7. moderate tempo
8. flat
9. sharp
10. fast tempo
11. tied notes

139

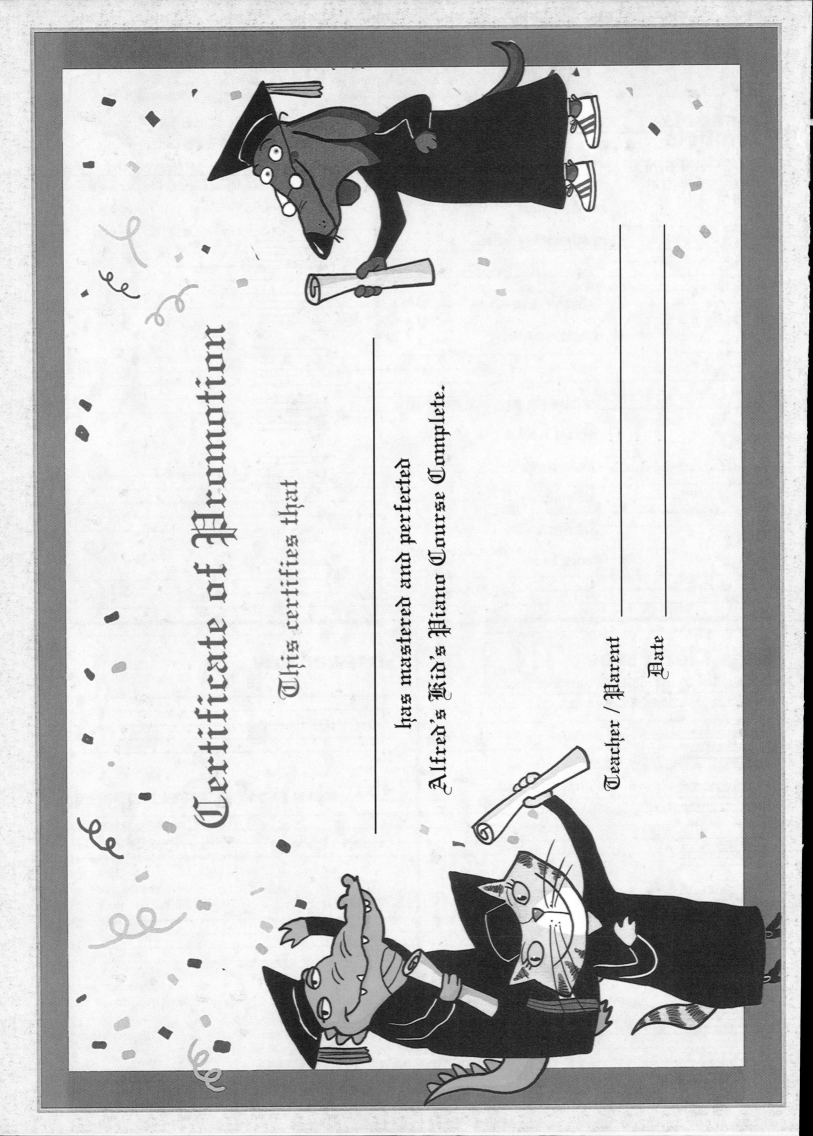

Certificate of Promotion

This certifies that

_____

has mastered and perfected
Alfred's Kid's Piano Course Complete.

_____
Teacher / Parent

_____
Date